The Triumphant Child

The Triumphant Child

A practical guide to raising two, three and four year olds

Edited by Olson Huff, MD FAAP and Nicole Rawson-Huff

To Jeanine,

with great appreciation for her concern and devotion to our children!

Sixty Second Parent™

Best wishes Olson Huff

ISBN: 978-0-9822841-1-7

Special thanks and acknowledgement to the brilliant content contributors Anne Oxenreider, Margaret Taylor, Kim Masters MD, Dr Ross Campbell, Susan Mims MD
Edited by Olson Huff MD, Nicole Rawson-Huff
Content co-ordination by Michelle Hutchison
Typesetting by Kirby Jones
Cover design by Tiam Whitfield
Editing by Jane Todd, Glenda Downing

This book is dedicated to all parents of preschoolers, who daily face the challenges and experience the rewards of raising their children.

Contents

Introduction

Olson Huff, MD

Raising two, three and four year olds can be both challenging and greatly rewarding. During these early years in their children's lives, parents have the opportunity to raise Triumphant Children who are resilient, have healthy self-esteem and concern for others which they will maintain throughout their lives.

Through two generations, I have been privileged to share in the lives of children. I have treated them when they were sick, sutured their cuts, set their broken bones. I have sat by their bedsides in the dark hours of the night, laughed at their jokes, and worried with them through their anxious and fearful moments. I have swelled with pride at their accomplishments and wept with tears of sadness when their lives have passed beyond my ability to offer a cure.

Through all these happenings, I have learned a great deal about children and those who care for them. One lesson stands out, and it is this: with rare exception, parents love their children. Parents want the very best for their children and seek in every way possible the guidance and support necessary to achieve it.

Finding that guidance is not always an easy task. The world is filled with all sorts of ideas about how to raise and care for children. A never-ceasing array of information, from the practical to the ridiculous, useful to annoying and understandable to incomprehensible, bombards parents to the point of near exhaustion. Ways and means to obtain accurate and timely facts about the health and development of children are clearly needed. That is why this book has been written and the website www.sixtysecondparent.com was developed.

Here, parents who seek to know what is best for their children will find answers that have been gathered from the most knowledgeable sources on health, practical parenting and child development from around the world. The information provided here is for moms, dads and grandparents as they go about their task of raising their children. It is easy to understand, applicable to each day's events, encouraging, and most of all, refreshing!

Of all the many words of information and advice given in this book, one word is very clear. That word is *love*. You who are parents and grandparents will learn many useful things as you read on, but only you can add that one ingredient that binds them all together.

I know you will because for at least two generations I have watched you do it. Now, enjoy what you find here, share it with others and continue to love those who look to you for all the joys life has.

CHAPTER ONE

About your child

Anne Oxenreider

As the parent of a young child, you need to develop a keen eye for the inevitable stages of growth and learning that occurs in two- , three- and four-year-old children. Watching and anticipating the growth stages of your child will create moments to celebrate what others might see as only childishness. You are your child's first teacher and your job at this point is to help your child as she matures to realize her fullest potential. She will eventually learn to run smoothly without you, but whether she gains self-confidence and agility at the same time largely depends on the loving and supportive home environment that you provide. Don't worry, I know that it may sound daunting. However, guiding your young child can be a triumphant, fun, delightful and creative task.

Your two year old

Physical – Gross and fine motor development

By two years of age, most children walk around independently and carry multiple objects in their arms. One of your jobs as a parent is that of a 'Physical Education' teacher. Watch your child begin to jump all over the place, walk up stairs without holding on to your hand, and walk on her tippy toes.

Your biggest task during this stage lies in making your child's environment safe for exploring. Large muscle development and strength develop best when your child has 30 to 60 minutes of outdoor play. A two year old needs time, and your encouragement, to climb, balance, and run. Help your child practice balancing on a low balance beam in order to gain confidence and a good comfort level with her quickly developing body. Beware, however, that your two year old may have many accidents because she is taking more risks. Young children need your watchful eye to prevent a serious accident, and they need your encouragement to bounce back into play after a minor misstep. Your child needs to get her wiggles out often. When the perpetual motion machine that is your young child has exhausted you, remember that she is fully engaging in her job of learning how to use one of her greatest assets, her body.

A two year old's fine motor development allows her to hold and eventually cut with scissors. She can grasp blocks well enough to build small towers. Her trusty gross motor skills will allow her to take great joy in knocking the blocks down time after time. She will enjoy using her hands to hold a large crayon and scribble, or to finger paint. Her fine motor skills will also make her particularly good at tearing paper and squeezing bottles, which can be a lot of fun if appropriately directed.

The duties of an art and pre-reading teacher are added to your job description. Art activities give little hands opportunities to experience textures, colors and even various temperatures; they foster imagination and creativity too. Remember that for young children art activities are about the process – not the product. You want to provide a time for your two year old to enjoy exploring and creating. You don't even have to save or post the masterpieces (okay, maybe a couple).

Language, speech and cognitive development

Language and cognitive development provide many opportunities for the 'watch and wonder' part of parenting a two year old. With language, two year olds follow simple instructions and progress from single words to using simple phrases. Make-believe play emerges. Enjoy it all, and maybe buy some crayon solvent. Your two's language will give you insights into her cognitive development. You may notice that she understands the idea of the absence of things by saying 'all gone' and the availability of things by saying 'more'. The average vocabulary of two-year-old children is around 50 words. Notice that she might replace 'r' with 'w' and say 'dwink' and 'wabbit'. Alternatively, she may leave off initial 's' sounds, saying 'cary' instead of 'scary'. Write some of these down or record your child. Our daughter is ten, and we still say things are 'very cary' from time to time at our house.

The reading teacher in you knows what to do in order to foster a love of reading in your child. Read aloud to your child often. I know she wriggles a lot; she doesn't have to be sitting in your lap with a cup of tea. Reading the same book over and over teaches your child a lot. If you point out different things in the story each time (colors, shapes, names of animals), she will begin to discover that books have multiple lessons. Her vocabulary will expand as new words are reinforced. Rereading a story to the point that your little one can 'read' parts of it back to you (or her teddy) and shows that she has internalized the story she's getting hooked.

Social and emotional development

The social and emotional development of your two year old gains complexity. He demands increasing independence (are you hearing 'no' and 'mine'?), but often imitates adults. He wants to make more choices but feels overwhelmed if given too many. Because he is able to anticipate what comes next, he needs routines at bedtime, drop off, and mealtime. Your two year old may experience emotional overloads that lead to tantrums. As embarrassing as it is to experience a temper tantrum in the grocery store, you need to remember that it is not personal – he is not trying to embarrass you. At two, he is not able to communicate effectively, yet he has a new awareness of what he can do. This is a recipe for frustrations to grow. It may seem like he falls apart because he has no more juice in his sippy cup; but more likely, he reached the end of a string of frustrations that he did not or could not express and resolve. Patience and consistent parenting techniques are a job requirement.

Two's frustrations can also erupt when in group play settings. A parent with a trained eye can prevent many of these situations. At two years of age your child engages in what is called 'parallel play'. This means that he naturally plays with another child by doing the same or a similar thing within an eye's glance of another young child. It is fascinating to watch the observational skills of children this age and to see how they use them to try new things. The problem occurs when there is only one of a certain kind of toy or activity. Two year olds often grab something out of another child's hands because they are eager to do what they have seen. As your child's teacher, you may like to prepare his play environment with clusters of similar toys (two pull toys or two cars) when he plays with other children. Of course, this cannot always happen and thus begins the long journey of 'learning to share'.

Mealtimes provide many opportunities for not only good nutrition, but they also help the child learn good behavior and feel like an important part of the family. Encourage your two year old to use his new words for good table manners. Watch his sense of security deepen as he puts out the dinner napkins or places the final toppings on the pizza. Food is a way to bond with your child and a way to develop social and emotional skills throughout his lifetime.

Practical tips for your two year old

Two year olds are active, creative and joyful! These littlies enjoy a bit of independence in their play. They love to actively manipulate objects in their environment and spend time thinking about how they work. Information about the environment is gathered by using all the five senses: seeing, hearing, tasting, smelling, and touching. To encourage your two year old's growth and development make sure her environment is full of interesting activities and toys.

- Two year olds are very energetic and active, they love rough and tumble play. Place a mattress on the floor and encourage your little one to roll, bounce and tumble.

- Set up a simple obstacle course in your backyard using a cardboard box for a tunnel, a skipping rope on the ground to walk and balance on, and a hula-hoop on the ground for jumping in and out.
- Play catch with your child. Start out with a beach ball and introduce smaller balls as your child becomes more skilled at catching and kicking. Teach your child how to roll a ball back and forth to you.
- Children this age take great delight in moving their bodies to the sound of music. Do not limit the choices to just children's music. For example, put on some fun rhythm and blues … the choice is yours.
- Have a few riding toys with wheels. This helps develop the muscles and coordination necessary for riding a tricycle later on.
- Put an outdoor play set with swings and a slide in your backyard.
- Encourage your child to thread large wooden beads onto string.
- Show your child how to turn doorknobs and how to use wind-up toys.
- Two year olds are just beginning to engage in make-believe play. Provide some toys such as pretend food, dress-up clothes, baby dolls and

accessories, small table and chairs, and a doll's stroller so your child can begin engaging in make-believe play.

- Toys that have switches, buttons, and knobs hold a strong fascination for children of this age. Some puzzles have all of these on them.
- They enjoy sorting shapes, colors and objects. Encourage your child to help sort the laundry; socks with socks, shorts with shorts and so on. Use colorful pegs and have your child sort them by color. Large threading beads and coloured blocks are great for sorting games.
- Two year olds enjoy simple puzzles with no handles as they are just beginning to understand the relationship of putting objects together that fit. Puzzles with two to three pieces are enough. Add puzzles with more pieces as your child becomes more skilled.
- Be creative with play-dough. Show your child how to roll it, squash it, and how to cut it. Provide a variety of cookie cutters and plastic accessories to extend the use of play-dough.
- Turn on some music and play Follow the Leader. Jump, skip, hop, and roll around on the floor, walk on tiptoe and clap your hands.
- Water play is perfect for this age. It produces a wide range of responses and holds a strong

fascination. Place a tub of water on an old shower curtain on the floor in the kitchen. Give your child a doll, some plastic containers and a few toys and encourage your child to wash them. You can also provide a range of pouring toys such as funnels, scoops, and small containers. Include a few objects that float. Poke holes in a margarine container so your child can watch the water dribble out. *Always* supervise water play – *never* leave your child alone, not even for a second.

- Sandboxes are fantastic. They are great for sensory development. Include some scoops, spoons, buckets, toy cars, and small shovels. (Remember to keep the sandbox covered when not in use to prevent cats from using it as a toilet.)
- One of the most important things you can do for a two year old is read aloud to him frequently. Not only does this build his vocabulary skills, but it also builds a special closeness between you and your child.

Suggested books for two year olds

(These titles are available at the online store at www.sixtysecondparent.com.)

Goodnight Moon by Margaret Wise Brown
Once Upon a Potty by Alona Frankel
Pat the Bunny by Dorothy Kunhardt

Peek-A-Who? by Nina Laden
The Very Hungry Caterpillar by Eric Carle
Love You Forever by Robert N. Munsch and Sheila McGraw
Wheels On the Bus by DK Publishing
Dear Zoo by Rod Campbell
A Potty for Me! by Karen Katz
Pumpkin Soup Book by Helen Cooper
Time for Bed by Mem Fox and Jane Dyer
We're Going on a Bear Hunt by Michael Rosen and Helen Oxenbury
My Big Animal Book by Roger Priddy
The Little Mouse, the Red Ripe Strawberry and the Big Hungry Bear by Don and Audrey Wood

Your three year old

Your contract as a parent educator has been renewed; you now have a three year old. All your previous duties remain the same. Your three year old needs a physical education, art and pre-reading teacher as well as a nutritionist–chef.

Physical – Gross and fine motor development

Your three year old may hop, stand on one foot for five or more seconds, as well as kick and throw a ball forward. She will take pride in her ability to walk up and down stairs without assistance. This is a good time to find a tricycle or other low-rider pedal toy. Another good gross motor play item is a beanbag. At our house, the dog became the moving beanbag target; luckily our little one did not have a good aim.

In terms of fine motor coordination, your child's dominant hand may emerge. Watch to see if this is happening to your child. She will use this preferred hand to work scissors and tear single pages in a book. Simple toys will serve her well. Peg puzzles require careful pinching and maneuvering; fat crayons allow for drawing big circles and squares; and a spray bottle full of water will give her hands a workout (and possibly clean the sidewalk).

Language and intellectual development

Some of the frustrations of being two subside as your three year old becomes capable of using words to express feelings. While your child has become cognitively capable of associating feelings with a word, he will need help from intuitive parents to label the feeling with the right word. When you see frustration building, say, 'I can see that you feel angry (or mad or upset)'. Be sure to label the positive emotions too. Be ready for the first time that your child expresses an emotion appropriately, and give lots of praise. You might say, 'Way to go. I know that you are mad but I am so glad that you could tell me that with your words'. Now is a good time to think back about times that you felt a certain emotion. Tell your child about a time that you felt the same way and how you handled it or what made you feel better. Knowing that you share the same feelings provides comfort and empathy.

Three year olds love to tell stories. He will not only ask many questions, he will also create long strings of events, saying 'and then', and 'next' often as he goes along. His stories will show that he has also developed a sense of time. He may correctly use yesterday, today, and tomorrow. You may also notice his awareness of colors and their names as he spins a tale. You can be a great parent educator by telling his stories back to him. By reflecting his words, you allow him to evaluate and appreciate his own story. It is also helpful to ask sequence questions too. ('What's going to happen next? Or tomorrow?') This will reinforce his developing sense of time.

Social and emotional development

The three year old's social and emotional world begins to expand beyond self. His social and emotional skills include following rules, using 'please' and 'thank you', and developing an understanding of what it means to take turns. Your child needs you to set limits and expect him to do things for himself – these are fundamental parts of getting ready for school. If you haven't yet, this is the right time to arrange for a regular play date or playgroup. He needs ample exposure to and practice with negotiating his play with other children near his age.

This age group often needs to learn to cope with a new baby. This presents a significant social and emotional challenge for a young child because of his strong attachment to his mother – he is only beginning to understand the concepts of taking turns and sharing. Allow your child to help make decisions about baby items; share with him ahead of time that it won't always be easy when the baby arrives and arrange special 'mommy' or 'daddy' times. Lastly, expect some regression in your three year old. Praise him when he does something grown up, like picking up the baby's bottle or toy, and let the throwbacks to old behaviors go by.

Towards the end of his third year, your child will also begin to develop a moral sense. In small ways, empathy begins and a sense of 'right' and 'wrong' begins to apply to other people. Your child needs you to be clear about your values. Simple statements such as, 'In our family, we always tell the truth', or 'The Smiths love the Earth and recycle' set a moral compass for your child. Take time to talk with other family members and friends about what they value. This is a good time to be intentional. Much like your previous parenting experience now is the time to catch your child in a good behavior and provide a lot of praise. Say, 'That's very thoughtful', when he makes a picture for someone else. On the other hand, plan for ways that your child can make something he does wrong right again. If he tears a page out of a book (hopefully not a library one), help him to tape it back in. If he hits someone, have him go get a bag of ice and apply it to the person he hit … sometimes saying 'I'm sorry' just isn't enough.

Practical tips for your three year old

Welcome to the wonderful and whimsical world of the three year old. This is a year full of developing skills such as riding and steering a tricycle. The first half of the year is generally calm whilst the second half can be a little tumultuous characterized by strong-willed behavior and a sense of emotional insecurity. It's a little similar to what is called the 'terrible twos'. Give lots of extra cuddles and love. Don't have the expectation that your child should always behave nicely. We all have our bad days! Here is a group of ideas and activities that three-year-old children tend to love and enjoy.

- There is no better way to calm a child than by bringing him in touch with nature. Take your child on a trail hunt in your backyard. Look for snail trails, busy groups of ants or tracks made by a cat, bird or dog. Discuss how many legs the animal has, what type of food it likes to eat and where it sleeps at night.
- For a child with a sudden surge of physical energy that needs to find a positive outlet, fill up a pillowcase with newspaper and throw or kick it to one another.

- Lay your child down on a large piece of butcher paper and trace around his entire body. Have your child color in the clothes and draw eyes, nose, mouth, and hair. Cut it out and hang it up.
- Add more supplies to your make-believe toys. New dress-up clothes, hats, oven mitts, kitchen utensils, and play food can really energize your little one's make-believe play. Join in and cook a meal together. Your child will *love* you for this.
- Your child can now understand simple instructions. You can help develop these listening skills by playing games such as Simple Simon Says.
- Choose puzzles with about five simple pieces. Put them together with your child and then encourage him to do them on his own. By helping your child in the beginning you help him avoid unnecessary frustration and giving in too quickly. Help build confidence that in turn builds skills.
- Provide a variety of colored paper and old magazines to use as cutting material. Children will need this skill, as they tend to do a lot of cutting activities. Therefore it is a good idea to develop this skill early on. Make sure you have child-sized safety scissors with rounded edges that are not too sharp).
- Give your child some simple chores to do. Putting away his clean clothes, dusting furniture, or

putting napkins on the dinner table are appropriate for this age. Chores encourage a sense of pride and responsibility.

- Purchase some paints and paintbrushes. While some painting will occur, expect that most of the time will be spent mixing the colors. This is great! It is how a child learns that when you combine yellow and blue you get green. Show him how color combinations create a new color. Expect a mess and avoid a clean-up disaster by putting an old plastic shower curtain on the floor to catch all the paint spills. Painting is a lovely experimental and relaxing activity for three year olds.
- Three year olds enjoy sorting shapes and colors, so having a shape-sorter on hand can be a good idea.
- Jungle gyms allow your child to practice climbing, jumping, and exploring. They even make a great cubby house.
- This age group loves musical instruments such as bells, triangles, and rhythm sticks.
- Simple games such as picture dominoes, matching and lotto are always enjoyed.
- Play-dough, finger-paint, and crayons are adored.
- Blowing bubbles is always a winner.
- Housekeeping toys such as a child-sized broom, mop, stove, and refrigerator encourage make-believe play.

- Wagons and a small wheelbarrow will keep energetic bodies busy.
- A baby doll and accessories will be much loved and cared for. Role-model how to care for a baby, by showing your three year old how to change a diaper, how to feed and bathe a baby.

Suggested books for three year olds

(These titles are available at the online store at www.sixtysecondparent.com.)

Bread and Jam for Frances by Russell Hoban
Curious George by H.A. Rey
Franklin in the Dark by Paulette Bourgeois
The Little Engine That Could by Watty Piper
Richard Scarry's Best Word Book Ever by Richard Scarry
The Very Hungry Caterpillar by Eric Carle
Alexander and the Terrible Horrible No Good Very Bad Day by Judith Viorst and Ray Cruz
Chicka, Chicka, Boom, Boom by Bill Martin Jr., John Archambault, and Lois Ehlert
Time for Bed by Mem Fox and Jane Dyer
Richard Scarry's What Do People Do All Day? by Richard Scarry
Jamberry by Bruce Degen
We're Going on a Bear Hunt by Michael Rosen and Helen Oxenbury
There Was an Old Lady by Pam Adams

Your four year old

A four year old will expand on the abilities developed over the past few years and develop new skills too. Much of what you need to focus on to prepare your four year old for her upcoming formal education focuses on building confidence within the developmental benchmarks listed below. A child needs to feel secure and positive about each area of her development in order to navigate her environment when she is away from you.

Physical – Gross and fine motor development

Your four year old's muscle strength, sense of balance, and coordination make her more independent. Her honed gross and fine motor skills allow her to use a fork and eat independently (you still get the cutting up firm food detail). She can dress herself and is likely to enjoy picking out her own clothes. In terms of gross motor abilities, you may see your child walking up and down the stairs with alternating feet, jumping over things with agility, and balancing on one foot. This would be a great time to set up a soccer goal in the yard or buy a set of large scarves for dancing to music. Your child's self-esteem grows as she experiences her body move and work effectively.

In addition to dressing and eating, your child's fine motor skills will allow her to use writing implements with greater precision. During this year, she will begin to copy letters and even write her first name in capital letters. Medium to large-sized interlocking blocks and lacing cards will allow for play-filled ways to build the muscle strength and coordination needed to write well. An easel with fat paintbrushes and thick markers will also do the job.

Language and intellectual development

A four year old uses language with greater complexity. She will use complex sentences in addition to the simple sentence constructions previously developed. She will have fewer pronunciation errors. She has a greater sense of words in general; she will greatly expand her vocabulary and want to know the meaning of words that she hears. She will use her word sense to tell complex stories that are more detailed, and to initiate conversations with adults. If you are in a habit of speaking baby talk to your child (it can be to show affection), start to break the habit. You and your child need to reinforce the language abilities that are forming in her brain.

At four, your child will count to ten and do very simple addition and subtraction. Her ability to recognize and name shapes expands to include triangles and rectangles in addition to squares and circles. At three, she could conceptualize yesterday, today and tomorrow. Now she will begin to recognize the cycle of a week and learn the names for the days of the week and the months.

Cognitively, your four's mind wants to know why. She sees the potential for cause and effect all around and will constantly ask you about what she sees. Your response is, as you have come to expect, important. You need to respond to her questions but don't always assume that you need to provide the answer. I find that preschoolers who ask 'why?' often have a theory of sorts in their head and are looking for confirmation. Ask the why question back, 'Sara, why do *you* think it is?' I often found that my daughter had a very good idea of why something was happening; and by asking for her thoughts, I gained insights into how she perceived the world around her. When it does feel appropriate to explain to your child, remember to use language and concepts that she already knows – creating a bridge between what she knows and wants to learn.

Social and emotional development

Fours are also gaining a better understanding of the causes of emotions. Their more complex language allows for a greater range of expression. Their motor skills allow them to expend tension and draw pictures of feelings. Their increased ability to play cooperatively provides them with models to either emulate or avoid. Fours are better able to ease in and out of social settings and play cooperatively. They will attach to certain friends as best friends and they, with encouragement, will use eye contact while talking to adults. You can support your child's social and emotional development with some good parenting fundamentals: allow him to make simple choices, set clear limits, provide consistent consequences for negative behaviors, and compliment both good behavior and constructive risk taking.

The total picture of a four year old's development adds up to school readiness. The sense of confidence in himself and empathy for others will serve him well in the classroom. By limiting TV and computer time and providing ample reading aloud time, you will foster his ability to listen to others and to concentrate for longer periods. As your child's first and best teacher, you will continue to foster his confidence as the formal classroom presents him with new challenges. Each area of your child's development provides an opportunity for you to experience the amazement of human life. Take a moment every day to celebrate and nurture the joys of your growing triumphant child.

Practical tips for your four year old

Hooray! You've made it to the fabulous world of the four-year-old child. Expect to be constantly asked, 'Why?' Four year olds are very inquisitive and want to know everything! They enjoy playing with other children their own age. Sharing, taking turns and cooperation are all behaviors that a four year old is now capable of doing. Exaggeration is normal and so is aggressive and obnoxious behavior with siblings. Praise your child often and be gentle when they make mistakes. Here are a few ideas on what your four year old might like to do.

- They love to talk and now have a vocabulary of almost 1600 words. Surround them with language: tell made-up stories, read riddles and stories and sing lots of songs. Make up silly rhyming words like, cookie, wookie, lookie. Four year olds really enjoy being silly and will get a huge sense of enjoyment out of saying silly things.
- Physical activity is vital to strengthen and develop muscles. Set up your backyard with enticing active toys such as swings, slides, and a jungle gym. A tricycle is excellent for this age. Balls of all sizes are good for playing throwing and kicking games.
- Help your child become an expert in learning concepts such as big and bigger. Ask simple questions such as, 'Which is bigger – a car or a bus?'
- Teach your child the names of her body parts.
- Use puppets to tell stories and encourage your child to do the same. This is a great way to enhance language development.
- Play riddle games such as, 'I have four legs, big ears, I live in the jungle, and people can ride on me. What am I?'

- Read books that have repetitive language. Before you know it, your child will be able to 'read' them to you.
- To help develop memory try asking your child at bedtime to remember two favorite things she did that day.
- Cook with your four year old. It's remarkable what they can learn: sequencing, how to follow directions, counting, and measuring.
- Four year olds have an amazing imagination. Tap into this resource by providing them with a variety of materials such as boxes, plastic containers, paper and glue. Start a useful box at home where you keep cereal boxes, used wrapping paper, milk cartons and so on so that your child has a bunch of interesting things to pull out to make a car, a rocket ship or even a boat. The sky's the limit when the useful box comes out.
- Building blocks are perfect for developing eye and hand coordination.
- A dollhouse is an excellent toy for this age, to help her re-enact daily life – be silly with it too!
- Provide your child with different types of paints, such as acrylic and water paints.
- Lacing cards and threading are super for enhancing fine motor skills and four year olds enjoy the challenge they provide.

- A sandbox is appreciated by this age – your child will love to dig and to create with sand. Have plenty of spades, buckets, digging trucks, and water.
- Experiment with puzzles that are more complicated. Find out which ones your child likes to do the best.
- Clay, play-dough, and finger paints encourage creative play.

Suggested books for four year olds

(These titles are available at the online store at www.sixtysecondparent.com.)

Are You My Mother? by P.D. Eastman
Good Night, Gorilla by Peggy Rathman
Sheep in a Jeep by Nancy E. Shaw and Margot Apple
The Relatives Came by Cynthia Rylant and Stephen Gammell
Night in the Country by Cynthia Rylant and Mary Szilagyi
Animals Should Definitely Not Wear Clothing by Judi Barrett and Ron Barrett
Rosie's Walk by Pat Hutchins
Five Little Monkeys Jumping on the Bed by Eileen Christelow
Curious George Goes to the Beach by H.A. Rey
Harold and the Purple Crayon by Crockett Johnson

Whoever You Are by Mem Fox
Quick as a Cricket by Audrey Wood
Where the Wild Things Are by Maurice Sendak
Barnyard Dance! by Sandra Boynton
The Grouchy Ladybug by Eric Carle

Anne Oxenreider

Anne Oxenreider's entire career is based around families and young children. She has a Masters degree in Education, as a result of her enthusiasm for preschool parenting. This passion has led her into numerous roles including that of grant writer for human service organizations, director of a community-wide preschool parent program, preschool teacher, mother, and foster parent. Her varied roles as an administrator, educator and parent are evidence of her enduring commitment to families and young children.

Building on this preschool parenting philosophy, Anne directed a preschool parenting project that funded local family centers and launched a multi-year preschool parenting campaign that included positive parenting messages on television, radio, fast food kid's meal bags, and other promotional items. Anne is committed to community work and has applied and won multiple private and state grants, receiving funds for family resource centers in her community. In addition, Anne worked with a community task force that launched a minority infant mortality reduction program.

Anne and her husband have had the privilege of foster parenting four preschool children and are beginning the process of foster-to-adopt a preschool child. Anne is currently the part-time director of a college writing center and working on a second Masters degree in English composition.

Recommended toys

Inquisitive and creative are two words that come to mind when thinking about the play life of a young child. They love to pretend play and copy what grown-ups do. They are also developing quite a bit of independence and know what they want to do. Organize toys into plastic containers using categories. A container for kitchen utensils and play food, another for dress-ups, and another for blocks. You get the idea. This way, when your child has an idea of what she wants to do, she can quickly find what she needs straight away and it makes your life easier too!

Here is a guide for toys that will educate and entertain your child:

- Building blocks – your child will be able to start building towers of increasing height.
- Puzzles – at this age your child will love to fit objects together. Doing puzzles becomes rewarding and challenging as she gains even more control over her fingers. Provide a variety

of puzzles. Puzzles that show a picture of an animal or an interesting scene (such as a farmyard) are perfect for this age.

- Threading beads – as your child becomes more skilled at this, find beads that are slightly smaller to keep her challenged. Always supervise bead play.
- Shape sorters – your child can handle small objects now with one or two fingers which means she can really experiment with placing objects into their correct holes.
- Dress-up clothes – children love to pretend. Provide dress-up clothes that are imaginative, such as fairies and wizards, but also include dress-up clothes that mimic real life people. Examples of these are construction workers, doctors, and nurses.
- CD player – to encourage your child's independence, provide a variety of CDs and a child-friendly CD player to encourage your child to develop her own taste in music.
- Tunnels – children love to crawl through these and they're great for using inside and outside.
- Duplo – these are fun for nimble fingers to use. Be sure to include some animals and people.
- Cars and trucks – a small collection of different vehicles encourages a range of play opportunities. Include dump trucks, a garbage truck, a car, a

farm truck/tractor and a fire engine. Boys and girls both enjoy playing with them. Find a small patch of dirt in your yard so your child can construct roads and towns.

- Animals – a collection of animals with a little barn is another way to encourage imaginative play.
- Puppets – you could include a few people, a couple of animals and a lot of imagination! Puppets are great for developing language and communication skills.
- A small table and child-sized chairs.
- Dolls and accessories, including doll's clothes, beds and strollers.
- Play-kitchen and utensils, plastic or wooden play food.

Toy safety

Make sure toys are safe for your child by taking a quick look at the following tips:

- Building blocks offer a multitude of learning opportunities for children. Check to make sure that your child's wooden blocks have smooth surfaces. Check that the paints and finishes on them are non-toxic. It can also be a good idea to model safe ways to play with wooden blocks by building with your child.

- Role-playing with dolls is a big part of play for children of this age. Be careful to select a safe doll. If the arms, legs or head can be removed, make sure that there are no sharp wires inside the body. The plastic needs to be quite soft, as hard plastic can break causing sharp surfaces or small parts to break off. Check that eyes and buttons cannot be easily removed. All clothing for the doll should have Velcro or clips to dress the doll. There should be no pins used at all. Check handbags and doll accessories to make sure they are safe and don't contain sequins or small pieces. Check your child's dolls regularly to see if any ribbons, buttons, or small pieces have become loose.
- Children love to play with toy cars and trucks. Choose ones made from durable material. Make sure that all the little parts such as windows, seats, and steering wheels are securely attached. Check metal vehicles for sharp pieces and edges. The wheels should be firmly attached, but if they do come off, make sure that they don't expose sharp axles or rough metal. Be careful when selecting dump trucks. Make sure little fingers can't be squashed when the tray is tilted and put down again. If the truck has a towing string, make sure that it is not long enough to fit around your child's neck.

- Fridge magnets are fun. However, if you have a young child under three in the house, magnets will need to be placed up high out of reach.
- Kites provide lots of outdoor fun. Follow these tips and make sure your next kite flying experience is a safe one. The kite shouldn't have any metal parts. It should come with the following safety label, '*Warning*: Do not use near overhead power lines.' Check the line of the kite and make sure it has no metal materials. Any metal can be a potential 'shock hazard'.
- Toy guns and pistols can be dangerous. They should have a barrel plug and be designed so children are unable to shoot out projectiles such as pens or pins. Always supervise these toys and tell your child never to aim at another person's face.
- Chemistry sets are very exciting, but you will need to wait until your child is over the age of twelve in order to be safe.
- Trampolines can offer hours of fun. Try to find one that has a net all the way around it and with an opening that can be closed to prevent children from falling out.
- Toy chests can be a good way to store your child's toys but they can also be a safety hazard. The American Academy of Pediatrics recommends the following safety tips for safe toy chest use: 'Make

sure they have locking supports and safe hinges, as well as ventilation holes.'

Final thought

This chapter has provided a lot of information (and hopefully encouragement) about your child's preschool development. However, you need to remember that children develop differently. The milestones found here are largely agreed upon, but cannot be predicted in each child in the right order or exact timing. Often a child's development comes in bursts. You may begin to look things up in books and worry and then in the next two weeks your child rockets forward. However, you do not need to worry alone if you begin to see uneven development in your child. Ask the professionals in your support network for an opinion. Often a day care worker or preschool teacher is the first line of response. Remember, most early childhood educators have seen hundreds of preschool children and will give you a candid response. Your child's pediatrician or a pediatric nurse may choose to have your child undergo professional developmental testing. Early intervention with delays often allows for on-time school readiness.

CHAPTER TWO

Parenting the triumphant child

Margaret Taylor

While parents navigate their way through the events of the day, thoughts about parenting their children spill into their conversations at work and lunch appointments with friends. Because parents don't get report cards, ideas and worries about being a good parent drive them to find useful answers that validate they are covering all of the right material. A parenting report card or annual review might be helpful. Learning basic parenting skills helps parents raise independent, emotionally healthy, triumphant children. Many people mistakenly assume that parenting comes naturally.

Children are constantly measured on their progress in school. Similarly, employers rate employee annual productivity and teamwork. Parents, on the other hand, are left to sort out their parenting know-how with whoever will listen, and hope that the advice they receive will lead them in the right direction. Adults are accustomed to and familiar with annual reviews and report cards because they provide a clear picture of success and achievement. We like to know when we are doing well and how we can do better. We have all received grades or endured performance reviews that may have described us as 'works well with others', 'uses time wisely', or 'solves problems'. Students also make developmental progress on several characteristics in learner profiles in order to move to the next level. A recent review of my kindergartener's report card was eye-opening in the vocabulary used to describe her behavioral profile. As a parent I wondered if I would be making 'satisfactory progress' on a 'parenting profile'? Basic skills profile the information from which moms and dads can draw, and put parents at ease about what they can expect as they prepare for the job.

How does a parent raise a triumphant child? A list of tried-and-true 'good parenting' skills follows in this chapter. Some parents cringe at the prospect of learning a list of skills, or trying to break old habits and actually get organized. The following list (and all lists) must be kept in perspective: communicator, risk-taker, educator, informer, thinker, and inquirer. As parents fall into each of these roles, they also must bring with them socially acceptable principles, along with a caring, open-minded, well-balanced, and reflective nature. Above all, they must try to maintain a good sense of humor. No one parent can possess all of these skills consistently, all of the time. A good parent reviews the profile of skills, tosses some of them aside to try later and then, most importantly, molds them to suit the pace of their family's life. The first step is just thinking about learning some essential skills. (Imagine the kindergartener who takes the first step into the classroom and decides to stay.) Our development as parents mimics the stages that children progress through to become independent, and as we guide them, we are learning how to be parents. Each day presents something new to both children and parents. Even with our basic instincts and background knowledge, the unexpected, sometimes raging, scenarios may throw us off guard and have us searching for answers, reinforcement, and gratification. In order to teach children how to communicate, care, inquire, respect, and value others, parents also have to communicate, care, inquire, respect, and remain calm too. When reading over a learner profile on a school report card, parents find it easy to see the common characteristics between kindergarten skills and good parenting skills:

- *Communicator* – listens and expresses feelings, works well with others.
- *Risk taker* – willing to make mistakes and eager to try new things and find solutions.

- *Knowledgeable* – seeks to learn more information about self and others and *uses* information.
- *Principled* – is honest and fair with a sense of justice.
- *Caring* – sensitive to needs and feelings of others and helpful.
- *Open-minded* – listens to and respects other people's views.
- *Well-balanced* – considers other points of view, has a sense of self, and is efficient.
- *Reflective* – thinks before acting and recognizes own learning strengths and weaknesses for growth.
- *Thinker* – uses prior knowledge, solves problems, seeks new ideas, and asserts self.
- *Inquirer* – wonders about other possibilities, and does not give up easily.
- *Sense of humor* – enjoys various aspects of learning and appreciates individuality. (This is not part of a real school profile, but seems essential for a parent profile!)

The traits listed above all characterize people who try to establish rules, communicate effectively, and develop a set of values with their children's future in mind. Possessing all of the above equipment will not produce perfect children, and it will not earn the parent a set of straight

A's. Instead, using these skills puts the parent in the driver seat on a long, bumpy road toward building a healthy relationship with their child. So, be *well-balanced*, *principled* and *caring*, and start enforcing some rules.

Rules

Rules show that parents care, and they teach socially acceptable behavior. For example, children need to know what rules to follow while playing at a friend's house, and how to conduct themselves with good manners. How do you communicate these rules? Specifically, outline before the playtime what behavior you expect when the time comes to leave: the child should be helpful and clean up, and properly thank their host. Whining or otherwise negative behavior will result in immediate consequences on their return home. Without clear limits, children will consistently and predictably repeat these undesired behaviors.

Other areas for which parents frequently establish rules include television, chores, appropriate language, mealtime, and bedtime. Parents must establish a set of rules to help children secure a position in the family, the classroom, and the community, but remember that being *well-balanced* and *caring* means keeping those rules in perspective. Parents are more effective when they recognize that rules may need to change as children grow and develop their own place in the world. Routines change, and children's perspectives on rules change. As children become more principled, they encounter more complex environments and groups of people, each with their own set of rules. For example, preschool rules, museum rules, and swimming pool rules all pose very different criteria to follow. Help children to decompress by having a sense of humor about all of the new rules that they have to learn. We can do this by providing simple examples of rules in the adult world by which adults must abide. Comfort them with the consistency of always being there for them whether they have figured out all the rules or not. After all, remember that parents are weaving a relationship, and must remain in control of keeping the child safe with a nice-fitting set of rules.

Rule guidelines

Childhood rules often seem unfair or confusing, So be *open-minded, think* and *reflect* on developing rules that make sense to a preschooler. Here are some memorable guidelines:

- *Rules should be age-appropriate and doable.* Notice that 'reasonable' is not a part of the equation. Attempts to reason with a preschooler often can lead only to frustration for both parent and child. Promote success for the child by keeping the rule within his known capabilities. For example, it is difficult (if not impossible) for a five year old to keep a tidy room all the time. But it is doable for him to pick up his toys, and put his shoes and clothes away before going out to play.

- *Rules should be simplistic.* A clear, concise explanation for why this rule is necessary should be enough for a preschool child to connect the dots between what is expected of him and how to produce that response. Safety is a very simple reason all children need limits, and it works well to explain why the many, many rules are necessary. The old-fashioned 'because I said so' asserts power, but falls short of providing a young child with the one-to-one correspondence of what might happen if he disobeys the rule. Instead, say, 'I want you to hold my hand in the parking lot because you are not tall enough for the car drivers to see you and that is unsafe. When we get to the car, you can let go and climb in.'
- *Be a coach rather than a referee.* Children need to learn how adults expect them to behave. They need a 'play book' for what to do when they team up with other kids. This is a difficult task to master if their grown-up just keeps blowing the whistle and yelling 'foul'. For example, if a child is hitting his classmate, try saying, 'Tell him why you

are angry at him so you can talk things out', instead of blurting out, 'Don't hit!'

- *Remain calm and repeat.* Expect the worst rebellion from the beginning, and learn to perfect the robot response. Consistently replying with the same simple explanation over and over equips parents to control any situation by deflecting their own anger or exasperation when faced with a screaming three year old.

Reflect

As our children grow, so must our parenting skills. With each grade or developmental stage comes new challenges that require adjustments and perspective. Does our established routine still work for my child and our family? How can consequences and communication be adjusted now that my child has moved closer to establishing some self-control and independence? Consistency doesn't mean forever, it merely suggests that with time we all learn how a new skill works for us ... it just takes practice.

Positive reinforcement and rewards

Report cards usually convey some sort of compliment like 'excellent', 'hard-worker', or even 'good effort!' Effective parents dole out the same reinforcement and rewards readily. Experts coin phrases like 'catch your child being good' to remind parents to seek out good behavior. To do this, you must be an effective *communicator* with both specific praise and body language (for example, hugs, smiles, thumbs up). Starter phrases that communicate this include:

- I like the way you …
- I'm proud of the way you …
- Good job on the …
- You were really patient or creative when you …

Consequences

What happens when it doesn't work? That is when we must resort to punishment and negative consequences. The *knowledgable* parent knows the differences between punishment and negative consequences, but may overlook the defining details. This does not mean we should design flip charts for every potential situation deserving a consequence. Choose behaviors that are important for the success of daily routines and socialization, and establish the negative consequences if they are not followed. The general idea is to naturally link tasks (put toys away) with privileges (go outside to play). This helps children learn responsibility for their behavior. Again, consistency is the key, which includes consistently *re-thinking* and *reflecting* on how the behaviors and consequences appropriately fit the family. Punishment, on the other hand, is associated more with intimidation, fear, and yelling, and often can backfire when the child adds yelling and bullying to his own behavioral repertoire. Often in counseling sessions with parents, it is evident that most parents resort to punishment when they have reached a dead-end. Parents get tired just as their kids do, and the meltdown ensues. The key for the parent is to recognize signs of distress (yelling and intimidating) and take their own time-out. This is easily done at home, and the surprise factor alone that mom or dad is taking a 'time-out' (somewhere in the house with supervision still possible) is enough to halt the child's misbehavior. The parent states that the child's misbehavior is so serious that they need some quiet time to *think* and *reflect* on the best solution. After all, the goal is for a smooth ride for all passengers, parents and children, even if the driver sometimes feels a little sick from all the commotion.

CONSEQUENCES – PARENT STORY

> **Antonija – five children aged seven, five, three, two, and six weeks**
>
> I have always tried to set sensible consequences for misbehavior, such as not eating dinner means no dessert, or fighting means time out. I try to make the consequences age appropriate. When I use time out, I use the 'one minute for each year' rule – that is my two

year old gets two minutes, my three year old three minutes and so on. Sometimes I use the questions of 'How old are you?' When they answer, I get them to tell me how old they think they were acting – they usually answer with a muffled 'two'. I also remind them that when they fight with each other or misbehave that their behavior hurts my feelings too.

Taking away privileges for favorite toys is something I also use, but not too often – these are the hardest to enforce. I feel like an ogre, but I know that boundaries and consequences are beneficial to the children's development – without them there would be chaos!

Communication

Sometimes in the monotony of the daily drive to work, or the commotion of settling children into their childcare for the day, effective communication gets lost in the rush. Prime opportunities always exist for encouraging open communication with your children, even in small slices of time, such as the time in the car on the way to work and preschool. The way we talk and listen to children greatly influences our relationship with them. Children learn how to express their needs, cope with problems, and respect authority through routine, small conversations with parents.

Communication guidelines

Here are some tips for starting small conversations that cover big ideas, and begin to shape the values children develop. A good communicator:

- Encourages with verbal and non-verbal cues. Children feel more welcome to talk when an adult stoops to their level and initiates conversation with a smile. Use praise and affection.
- Works as a team. Children need a play book on how to negotiate new surroundings and people. Coordinate consistency between a child's caregivers to help make learning important family values and behavioral expectations easier.
- Gives full attention. Children are always watching adults. Their observation skills are keen because their verbal skills haven't taken over yet. Turn off the radio or DVD player, and listen when your child speaks. Give her time to finish a thought, and make eye contact (if you aren't driving). The timing of her important questions won't always be convenient. Most experts agree that the most 'teachable' moments are spontaneous, casual opportunities. For example, if the preschooler pops the question about where her new baby sister will come from on the drive to school, it is

to the advantage of the parent to give full attention to laying the groundwork for future, less embarrassing discussions.

- Is honest. The easiest answer may be, 'I don't know, let's find out together.' Remember, parents get good grades for being *inquirers* too. Reminding children that grown-ups don't know everything and sometimes have to figure it out too gives children key problem-solving skills and permission to make mistakes. Having a *sense of humor* about our own shortcomings also relieves tension and provides us with a great way to laugh with our children.
- Sets aside alone time to talk. Other important parenting responsibilities often steal away individualized time with and attention to our children. Just as setting aside time each week is important to stay on top of big assignments at work or school, it is equally as important to the parent–child relationship.
- Encourages and respects children's opinions and feelings. Try to remember that children perceive problems and conflicts differently. They do not have the years of experience that we have and more importantly, they lack the verbal skills to express emotions. Encourage and model for your child how to express feelings; for example, 'I need to make sure I understand. You're sad because … '

Or, 'You seem really upset. Did something happen at day care today that did not go your way?' Repeating, identifying emotions, and clarifying questions invite children to speak up, and to consider the impact of their words and feelings on others.

COMMUNICATION – PARENT STORY

Ingrid and Brad – two children aged eleven and two

My husband and I have always had very different parenting styles. Brad has a very traditional style (he tends to see things in black and white with no shades of grey), on the other hand I am a bit of a softy and tend to give in a little more. We have had to work on this over the past eleven years. We try to work as a team so our children are not confused.

It has been hard at times – sometimes I don't agree with the way Brad has disciplined one of the girls and can't say anything until after the event.

We always try to catch up about issues we don't agree upon, in order to work out what we will do next time.

Knowledge

Extra credit is a convenient way for students to get ahead. It requires some extra work, but the rewards are evident in a glowing sense of accomplishment. Parents who squeeze in a little extra credit reading, even if it's only a momentary glance at reading a parenting brochure or magazine in a pediatrician's waiting area, find themselves better prepared. While parents learn over time that no two parents go about parenting in the same way, they also learn that no two children develop at the same rate. However, the developmental stages that all children go through are important for parents to know so they can guide their children's development and be aware of potential problems. During the infant to preschool years, parents need to know foremost that children lack self-control. It is apparent on short trips, while grocery shopping, getting dressed, and meal times that young children do not like to wait. Instead, they are curious explorers who aim to find out everything about the new world they live in. Young children have no boundaries unless parents set them. Parents guide their children best in this stage by arranging for a safe home environment where children know where they can play, eat, and sleep without breaking anything or hurting themselves. They also model manners like politely greeting the babysitter with a 'hello'. Simple expectations and a routine for their playtime, mealtime, and bedtime help children feel safe and successful. Once a child realizes where and how he fits into his environment, he can move on to more independent social relationships.

The stage from five to twelve years brings more independence and socialization. Children are eager to try things out on their own and go beyond the safe environment of the preschool years. They encounter more complex feelings beyond the safe boundaries at home (such as right versus wrong moral dilemmas), thus they need parents as a safety net to support and explain new challenges. We guide our children best in this stage when we give age-appropriate responsibilities, such as making a sandwich, using proper social etiquette, and picking out clothes to wear. These basic life skills help children gain the confidence and competence they need to conquer new school and social environments.

KNOWLEDGE – PARENT STORY

Jane and Mikel – four children aged six, four, two, and ten months

The minute you conceive there are literally millions of people out there, often complete strangers, who will offer you advice on how you should do things when you become a parent. My advice to new parents is, 'Listen to it all and then do what makes sense to you and what feels comfortable and what works.' For example, putting your child to sleep ... if you want to rock your child to sleep and you are happy doing it – great. If you want to, give your child turns at controlled crying and if you can cope with that – great. If you want your child to fall asleep at the breast and then pop her into bed – go for it. Do what works for you until either it doesn't work or you have had enough. However, don't feel guilty or think you are doing the wrong thing. There is not a first time mom or dad who doesn't have a hilarious story about how they used to get their first child to sleep. If you have a second child, you very often don't do the same things.

I used to rock my daughter to sleep and have Enya playing right outside her door. My husband and I did this for almost two years until number two child came along and we just couldn't keep it up. We were amazed at the fact that if our daughter cried a little and the new baby did the same they would put themselves to sleep, fairly quickly. With number three and four child, I would feed them, burp them, wrap them, give them a kiss and a cuddle and then walk out of that door when they were in their crib. I didn't have the time to rock them, and yes … they went to sleep.

Parenting skills summary

Most parents hope to see their children grow to be happy, considerate, and independent adults. The keys to effective parenting are not entirely found in any article, chapter or website. We must test-drive an array of parenting strategies and find a comfortable fit. The following list summarizes the effective parenting strategies up for review in this chapter (remember it is just a list, not an evaluation):

- Establish rules and show that adults care.
- Use positive reinforcement such as praise, affection, and rewards to foster self-esteem.
- Employ negative consequences to teach responsibilities and values.
- Communicate with children using undivided time and attention, and listening.
- Model and abide by the values that are important in the family.
- Understand normal child development milestones, and when to seek help.
- Make time for yourself in order to maintain a healthy outlook.

This list does not comprise everything that must be done to be a good parent. Sometimes it is even better to forget the list to avoid getting lost in the schedule of planned events and interventions.

PARENTING SKILLS – PARENT STORY

Jane and Mikel – four children aged six, four, two, and ten months

I constantly think about my journey into motherhood, and how it has changed with each child. Before we have children, many of us have a preconceived idea of what we will and won't do with regards to our parenting. Then we have a child and many of these ideas can just fly out the window. I remember thinking that I would never feed my children in the car – they could eat at appropriate times. Then I had my first child and boy oh boy, I was handing that food back faster than you could imagine. Many times, I had to feed her in the car because it was close to her sleep time – she would eat in the car and then I could pop her straight into bed, economizing time and not having her overtired.

Now, with four children, I am still handing that food back like there is no tomorrow and my car looks like a living compost. The children are happy and we have a calm journey (mostly). I always feed them good food – never junk!

Conclusion

As parents, we are only in the driver seat for a small speck of our child's life, and we can't forget to enjoy the drive. There really is no one 'right' way to parent. Our passengers in the car are constantly redirecting us and barking out new demands! Maps, guidelines, and a barrage of parenting information points eager parents in the right direction, but often leaves them reliant on the navigation system, rather than encouraging communication with the passenger. This parting example is mindful of keeping it all in perspective:

> The party guests are set to arrive in ten minutes. Where is the three year old? No-one can find her. The dining room is immaculately decorated with precisely placed ornamental Dora the Explorer tableware and a Dora cake as the centrepiece. The birthday girl was last seen wandering around in the house in a pull-up. The plan was for dad to make sure she was dressed for her party, while mom dressed herself. Obviously dad was 'googled' away at the computer again, and not in line with the routine. Grandma finds her and gasps, 'Oh my!' exemplifying the joy of grandparenting and choosing to wait and see what unfolds. Mom sighs a great big 'everything is ruined' sigh thinking that all of the party planning hours and preconceived sweet birthday memories are ruined. Dad, keeping his eye on the prize, runs to find the camera. He captures the real prize: a birthday photo of the pampered princess perched front and center on the dining room table with icing and cake splattered all over her cute little chubby body.

All parenting skills aside, Dad made the highest grade on this day because he kept a personal perspective on his job. He was not exactly following the routine or schedule, but he made up for that by living in the moment and keeping his eye on his cake-covered passenger. Whether it is whipping out the camera at an opportune time, or wearing a tearful smile and confidently saying, 'I'll be back soon' at preschool or day care, parents make extraordinary, split-second decisions every day that produce lasting impressions and memories. That decision-making ability does not come from studying and preparing extra-credit parenting homework assignments. The knowledge is gleaned from the bumpy, sticky ride of trial and error and suppressing the guilt we sometimes tow along when we make the wrong turn. We should not become obsessed with the notion of parenting by the book. Parenting is not necessarily one set of skills we possess for evaluation. Parenting is the most important part of our lives, and the availability of effective parenting skills at our fingertips keeps us safe and secure for the journey that lies ahead.

Margaret Taylor

Margaret Taylor holds a Master of Education in Counseling from Clemson University, and a Bachelor of Arts in Psychology from Davidson College. She is a nationally certified counselor and has worked as a licensed professional counselor for eight years in a variety of settings including public mental health treatment, private residential treatment and private practice. Her primary focus as a counselor has been with children and parents coping with emotional problems related to grief and trauma. For the last nine years, her focus has been on parenting two children with her husband in Mount Pleasant, South Carolina.

CHAPTER THREE

Routines

Nicole Rawson-Huff

Routines act like a general 'road map' to daily living. They provide a predictable sequence of events that allows a young child to feel safe and secure. This predictability helps the child to anticipate when events will happen, for example, after dinner we have a bath, brush our teeth, read stories, and then off to bed.

Imagine if you didn't have a clue about what was going to happen in your day. As adults, we have the luxury of being in the driver's seat for the better part of our day. We know when we'll eat breakfast and even what we'll have, we know when we'll go to bed and we know what we're going to do next. All of this planning and knowing gives us a sense of comfort and enhances our enjoyment of the day. For young children someone else plans most of these things for them.

Repeated positive daily experiences provide a strong feeling of security. From routines, children learn what to expect from their surrounding environment and how to understand the world they live in.

Daily routines help children understand what will happen in their day. It gives them a sense of order – morning, noon, and night – which helps them know what is coming next. Knowing what's going to occur throughout a day reduces stress and anxiety in young children. In a nutshell, it allows kids to relax and enjoy their day. They know they can trust that they will have their basic needs met. Food will arrive at predictable times, naps and sleep take place at certain times, and regular social events such as attending a playgroup happen every Wednesday morning. If you think children aren't aware of these daily routines, try mixing them up sometime! Your kids will let you know in record time what should be happening next!

Here are a few more advantages of routines:

- They encourage cooperation, as children know what is expected of them and what is will happen next.
- Children are more inclined to listen and do. Parental nagging is cut down, as children know that after dinner we clean up, read stories, brush teeth, and go to bed. This is just what we do to finish off our day. Once prompted to start these routines, children 'fall' into the habit of following them.
- Children gain a strong sense of independence. Daily routines encourage children to take care of

themselves. After a while, children will learn to dress themselves, brush their hair, make their own bed, and do simple chores all on their own if it's built into their daily routine.

- As children become older, they gain a feeling of confidence and mastery over these simple daily routines. Confident and independent children exhibit more cooperative and positive behavioral patterns.
- Routines allow children to gain skills in anticipating events. If you swim every Thursday morning, your children will learn this and look forward to this event.
- Routines create a healthy structure and encourage all family members to stick with it. If you establish healthy parameters around eating, TV, playing, resting, and being active you're more likely to adhere to them and not give in or settle for less.

Routines needn't be too rigid, flexibility is needed so your children will learn to adapt and adjust to those hiccups that inevitably happen: the scraped knee right as you are ready to step out the door, the phone call in the middle of story time, or the unexpected visitor at bedtime. React to these hiccups with calm and ease and so will your young child. Flexibility and adaptability are marvelous survival tools to teach children.

When creating a routine for your children, try to take into account the type of temperament your child may have. Temperament is innate. It's not something your child chooses – your child arrives in this world with his temperament already in place. It influences how your child experiences daily life. For example, some children arrive at a birthday party or playgroup and immediately dive into the thick of social happenings while another child may hang back for a while to observe and watch before joining in. Some children won't feel overwhelmed by a busy shopping mall while others will find all the sounds, smells, activity, and people too much to handle. Figuring out your child's temperament can help you be a more effective parent and create loving routines appropriate for your child.

You probably have a good idea about how your child reacts to changes in routines. Some children are simply more sensitive and find it hard to adapt. These 'routine lovers' are easily identified as they react to even the smallest of changes. A slight change in a bedtime routine or a different food on their dinner plate will upset their delicate equilibrium. These children literally thrive on predictability and order. They need it to feel safe, secure, and loved. On the flip side, we have the easy to adapt children who tend to quickly take to new foods, adjust easily to changes in routine, and find new things exciting and fun. These children quickly become accustomed to wherever you take them. As babies, they fed quite easily in busy and noisy environments and played happily wherever you went.

Most children are actually a mixture of both of these temperaments. They'll swiftly adjust to a new food but take ages to get used to a new place. They may make friends rapidly with children their own age but hold back in the presence of an unknown adult. The majority of children do get used to change if they are made to feel safe and secure within the loving guidance of a good daily routine.

Let's take a look at a few parenting strategies for the different types of temperaments. Parenting strategies depend heavily upon routines. For the children who are 'routine lovers', make good use of prompts before a change occurs in a routine. For instance, if your child is engaged in playing something and is very involved and you need to go to the store, give him a five-minute warning to allow him time to transition away from his play. Always get eye contact and a verbal agreement when conveying the prompt. You want your child to hear and take in what you have said. By doing this your child will become familiar with this finishing 'routine' and will learn to transition more easily. Whenever you are making a transition during the daily routine, such as going to day care, make use of a favorite toy. These favorite toys act as a transitional object to help a child ease into the next part of his day. Encourage your child to take an active role in making the transition. If leaving for day care or preschool, have your child help to gather his bag and shoes. Always praise your child when he successfully makes a transition, as this will help him build a sense of confidence.

For children with the temperament that 'goes with the flow', it's important to offer a variety of different activities and environments. Try a new park, attend a playgroup, and offer a wide variety of foods. Never assume that your child is okay with all changes. These adaptable children can be taken for granted. Watch and observe him in new situations and look for signs of possible stress and offer extra support when needed.

Several areas within daily living require routines. A basic guide would be shopping, bathing, bedtime, mealtime, preparing to leave for preschool or day care, and dressing. You may think of some others but these are the most common areas where routines are a good idea.

Routines that have been lovingly created with your child's personality and temperament in mind will go a long way in creating a triumphant child – one who is happy, healthy, and confident. So go ahead, put a little structure into your day, and reap the rewards!

Nicole Huff

Nicole is an honors graduate with a Bachelor of Science in Child Development and Family Relations, from Western Carolina University, Cullowhee, North Carolina. For many years she practiced in the field of child development in Asheville, North Carolina. Nicole is a certified 'parents as teachers' educator, which empowers parents to build the skills necessary to help children make the most of their crucial early-learning years.

She trained as a Child Life Specialist at Johns Hopkins Hospital in Baltimore. Nicole is also a certified facilitator for 'raising kids with special needs'. She has joined a number of projects supporting parents of children with special needs around the world. Nicole has been the founding manager of TotLine, a 24-hour, seven-day-a-week, parent information phone line. She is currently working with the International Program of Psycho-Social Research (IPP-SHR), which documents the experiences of children and adults who have lived with a serious illness (physical and mental). IPP-SHR has examined areas such as birth, palliative care, hematology–oncology, pediatrics, and spirituality. Nicole has co-authored over eight international publications and is currently the production officer of the *Psycho-Social Update Quarterly Review*.

Morning routines

Creating a rhythm or routine to the morning becomes vital as children grow older and begin to attend school or day care. A morning routine is your insurance that you will get out the door on time with all the necessary supplies for the day ahead. The key to avoiding morning madness is *organization*. Here are some tips to help your mornings become more organized:

- Prepare as much of the school, work, or day care supplies as possible the night before. Make lunches, pack bags with supplies, and organize clothes.
- Have your child choose her clothes the night before. This includes socks and shoes.
- Encourage your child to get dressed before she has breakfast (unless she is a very messy eater).
- Allow for about an hour in the morning to get everything done. An hour allows for the inevitable mishaps and hiccups that occur when getting a young child ready. It also allows you enough time to see if your child is healthy and well enough to go about her daily activities. If you rush too much in the morning, then a child who isn't feeling well can get caught up in the momentum and may be overlooked.
- One family I know plays a CD in the morning – for each song they need to complete a task: get dressed, brush teeth, make bed and so on.
- To get your child mentally and emotionally ready for the day, chat with her throughout the morning about the activities she might be doing at school or day care.

- If you have enough time left, sit down quietly together on the couch and read a short story or talk together – it's a nice way to connect before you go your separate ways for the day.
- Encourage independence in your child by having her make her own bed, get herself dressed and brush her own hair. (A child under three years will still need to be 'coached' on doing these tasks to help her out until she gets the hang of it.)
- Factor in the time it takes your child to gather her bag, get to the car, and buckle up. We all make the mistake of waiting until the last minute and then make a mad dash for the car and leave in an unnecessary frenzied rush!
- Remember, stay organized, stay calm, and leave your house happy (if you can) and you will have a positive start to the day.

MORNING ROUTINES – PARENT STORY

Monique and Chris – two children aged six and three

Getting ready in the mornings has been a constant battle with my older child. During the last three years, I have been a full-time university student. My husband either goes to work very early or works away, which means I am the one who needs to get the children ready. Getting the two children and myself ready in the morning and out

the door on time was achieved initially by making a game of it. I found myself taking on the role of playing the 'hairdresser' to get hair done, the 'shop assistant' to get her dressed, and the 'food store owner' to get the lunches made. This made it fun for my daughter and I found it a more stress-free way to get her ready in the morning. My son was the opposite – he would just get up, get dressed, and be ready on time without a fuss.

Other strategies I use to be on time include:

- Packing their backpacks the night before – this includes reading any preschool notices and making sure they have everything they need.
- Lunches made the night before – I put together their lunchboxes with everything in them except the sandwich, which I make in the morning.
- Ironing clothes the night before.
- Making sure I have all of my books and papers I need for university organized the night before.

Bedtime routines

Families function at their best when there are predictable routines in their day-to-day lives. For example, if a bedtime routine always consists of bath time, putting on pajamas, brushing teeth, reading stories, then bed, children will learn that 'this is what happens in our family' and will be less likely to resist.

Regular bedtime routines also help children to feel safe and to understand the behavior expected. Young children are learning new things every day. It is comforting for them to have times in their day when they know what is going to happen.

Bedtime routines also make life easier for you. If everyone knows what to do there will be less nagging, reminding, and hopefully less complaining and pushing of boundaries.

Setting up a bedtime routine

Here are some suggestions for establishing a bedtime routine. Firstly, think about all of the things that you need to achieve during a bedtime routine and make a mental list or, better yet, write them down. Your list may include bath, brush teeth, stories, toilet, prayers or songs, and bed. Of course you will decide the order and what to include. You will also need to think about what happens before bedtime. A late dinnertime or a child who eats slowly will affect when the bedtime routine starts. To make the bedtime routine a calm and unhurried affair you may need to consider having an earlier dinner.

You can also ask yourself, approximately what time does my child actually fall asleep? How long does it take him to get to sleep after he goes to bed? Some children fall asleep the minute their heads hit the pillow, others need a little 'processing time'. If your child needs around

30 minutes to wind down once he is in bed, you may need to get him into bed a little earlier.

All of this information will help you to decide roughly what time you need to get started. Taking everything that needs to happen into account, and your children's going to sleep style, make sure you are getting started early enough. Trying to hurry tired children does not make for a peaceful bedtime for anyone.

Here is the sample routine for a four-year-old child who takes approximately 15 to 20 minutes to fall asleep:

5.30 pm Dinner
6.00 pm Bath/pajamas
6.30 pm Stories/toilet/brush teeth
7.00 pm Bed and songs or prayer
7.10 pm Kiss and goodnight
7.30 pm Hopefully asleep

Take a few minutes to write down what a bedtime routine might look like for your family. All families are different. It may take a bit of experimenting to find the routine that best suits your situation.

Having children of different ages can be a challenge. Some parents like to put the younger child or children to bed first, others use two parents to divide and conquer, and others have older siblings help the younger ones.

Remember that all families are different; they also change and grow. What works when your child is two may not be appropriate when he is four. The challenge for the parent is to revise and check if the routine is working on a regular basis.

BEDTIME ROUTINES – PARENT STORIES

Helena and Joe – one child aged four

We have a basic routine we started when Alice was a baby and we try to stick to it, although now she is four she seems to be able to handle a few changes now and then. After dinner she has a bath and puts on pajamas, her father or I read two books usually on the sofa (this is the hardest bit to stick to as she always wants us to read more), then it is teeth, toilet, and bed. When she is in bed we put the night light on and sing a couple of songs, then kiss her goodnight. We have a little thing we say each night as we close the door: 'Goodnight, I love you … see you in the morning.'

Jane and Mikel – four children aged six, four, two, and ten months

As we now have four little ones and I have mostly been locked away feeding the baby at bedtime, we have set up a roster of activities for each night of the week so that it is easier for us to put the three other children to bed in a calm manner. For example, Wednesday night we draw and the children all have a drawing activity, which they do with one parent. While they are happily involved we take the youngest to bed with a story, then a little while later the next oldest, and then our eldest last. As we put them into bed, if they are under four, we sing them a special song, and then when they reach four they get a special verse – when they reach six they get an additional verse. They have to wait for these age landmarks and they know that it is a very special time when their turn comes. If they are extra fussy or boisterous, then we light a special angel candle, which they take to bed as we sing.

Jen and Rich – two children aged five and three

We have been working on the bedtime routine for about five years. Every time we think we've got it all worked out, our older daughter enters the next stage without telling us and we are left holding the pieces and trying to figure out what is happening. When she was younger, we would play the same CD every single night at bedtime to help queue up the idea that it's time for peace and quiet now. That wonderful CD is called 'On a Starry Night', and I still play it for my girls sometimes for old time's sake!

Mealtime routines

In today's fast-paced society, families often abandon eating together. Research shows that children who eat with their families are more likely to try new foods, make healthier choices, and even do better in school! Meal times are an opportunity for parents to strengthen their family, model good eating habits, and keep track of their children's lives.

As with the bedtime routine, provide enough time to make meal times unhurried. Take into account how long your children need to eat meals; this will help you to decide when the meal should be served. Mealtime routines are one of those routines that have a knock-on effect on the rest of the day. If it is a preschool day, and you offer breakfast too late, your child may not get finished or you may be late. Also, remember that dinnertime has an effect on when the bedtime routine can start.

Discuss with your partner what rules and rituals are important for your family at mealtimes, remembering to take into account children's ages or developmental stages. You may decide that children must remain seated during the meal or that everyone participates in a blessing – be realistic – expecting a three year old to master a knife and fork is probably asking too much.

Here are some suggestions for creating mealtime routines for your family:

- Try to plan one meal a day in which everyone can be together. If both parents are not available, have at least one parent eat with the children. If the weekdays are too hectic, make a special effort on the weekend.
- Focus on your children and try not to discuss adult issues. Start a tradition by having children share the best thing that happened to them that day. Enjoy your amazing family.
- Turn off the TV! Television viewing during dinner stifles conversation. Research shows that families that watch television during dinner eat more fatty foods and less fruit and vegetables.
- Let the children join in the mealtime routine. Children as young as two love to help! They can help prepare dinner (sprinkle cheese, chop bananas for fruit salad), set the table, or even do the dishes (if you don't mind the mess).
- At meal times model good manners, healthy eating, and a willingness to try new foods. Children will mimic your attitudes toward food. If you don't eat your vegetables, why should they? Be open to new ways of cooking too.
- Keep meals simple and be realistic about the amount of food that you give your children.

Jane and Mikel – four children aged six, four, two, and ten months

The children take turns bringing a lighted candle to the dinner table. We then sing a blessing. If the children are a bit fussy about coming to the table, I sprinkle some magic fairy dust and polish their seats. This tends to work because of their ages. At our house, we have a compulsory salad at the start of our meal, and the children know that it is the most important part and that it must be eaten before getting anything else. We have always been consistent with this and rarely have an issue with non-eating. If they are teething or overtired, then they just do their best.

CHAPTER FOUR

Challenges

Olson Huff, MD

Foot stomping is one way to say, 'I'm here!' Well, maybe not just to say, 'I'm here,' for contrary behavior may be a response to any number of happenings or for a variety of reasons. Young children may react vigorously when corrected, scream with frustration when denied, cry out when angry, or even become defiant when they are afraid. Such actions and tiring behaviors point to a number of developmental issues that help shape a child's temperament and are well worth examining.

First, there is the assertion of power. Viewed as defiance or belligerence, a young child's attempts to define himself may well be totally misunderstood. The underlying value of the emerging strength that defines character, self-reliance, and eventual problem solving is easily missed if only the behavior is noticed. True, it isn't easy to stop in one's tracks and declare, 'Great, we are having a character building moment,' when your child is screaming at the top of his lungs! However, seen in the larger scope of life, that is part of the reality that is unfolding – your child is learning about what it is to be triumphant.

What, then, is a parent to do when their child is creating such a ruckus?

That question leads to some other important insights. It may not seem so, but when a child has the so-called 'screaming fits', he may be very frightened by his own outbursts. While a defiant 'No!' represents power on the one hand, it surely must bring forth a sense of insecurity and the feeling of being out of control on the other.

Here then are two polar opposites to be found in the same expressions of behavior. These opposites are part of the struggle to comprehend what effect actions have on the immediate environment, and what reassurances can be gained that someone else is, thankfully, in control.

Defiance is seen in almost every step a child takes, from first words to kindergarten, and as a marker of independence and individual worth. It is the kind of behavior one notes in the so-called 'terrible twos', when defiant attitudes and foot stomping behaviors repeatedly accompany 'No!' It is also seen in the patterns of children who move from grabbing toys to sharing and from screaming to laughing. These are the times of testing and should be recognized as such. The emphatic 'No!' should be welcomed as a sign of testing, challenging, and defining. Like an echo from a mountain top, these actions play over and over to help children measure the limits of their own will and to respect the same in others. It is an incredibly powerful tool of growing up!

A common problem in raising children through these two- to four-year-old times of very expressive behavior is to err too far on either side in responding. An aggressive and angry parenting style can be even more frightening to a young child than their own outburst and may increase the frequency of such behaviors. On the other hand, the permissive parenting style with no attempt to correct or guide rowdy or belligerent behavior leads to repetitive outbursts of demanding energy that may become ugly and more and more difficult to redirect.

Therefore, what we have in defiant, testing, questioning, foot stomping, and aggravating activity is the expression of power that is waiting to be channeled. 'No!' on the part of the young child is an exhibition of the will to be a real person and the strength to claim that distinction. 'No' on the part of mom or dad is a marker that channels the testing into learning and the defiance into cooperation. Growing children have a great deal of strength and they need to test it. Wise parents recognize this to be so and are fully aware of their own strength to create a caring, positive, and sensible atmosphere of response.

So the question once again is, 'What is a parent to do?'

I suggest taking a bit of time to think through all the aspects of that question. Who, after all, is really in charge? How is a parent's power, which comes both from experience and from the desire to express love, best used? When is intervention necessary and when is it wise to let an outburst run its course?

Just as important as it is for the young child to gain definition of personal strength and deal with his own power, so it is with those who love and care for him. 'No!' sits in the middle of a two way street. Children do not learn the limits necessary to honor their own strength or move their self-perception from tenuous to confidence, in a vacuum. Parents, too, must know the power of their own ability to say no. The difference between the two lies in the ability to simply honor each other's presence and space. The developing child states his case loudly, perhaps angrily, and with the conviction that he must be heard. The parent – older, wiser, and calmer – can also say 'No' firmly and with conviction. What often occurs, however, is that a parent reacts rather than responds, upping the ante for the now nearly belligerent child and a war of wills begins that more often than not results in victory for neither side.

Here are a few simple suggestions for when outbursts become tantrums:

- Be sure that your child is safe from physical harm.
- Don't try to stop a tantrum but, rather, just keep your child close and secure.

- If there is another child involved, separate them.
- After all is over, some talk about feelings or what happened may be in order but make it simple.
- Don't threaten, bribe, cajole, or waffle. Be firm and calm, and don't be afraid to say 'no'.

Depending on temperament, beginning around eighteen months or so, children will begin to show a certain amount of self-defining spirit. That is good. Parents and caregivers help it grow by providing safe, predictable, and caring responses. The outcome eventually becomes one of comfortable independence and behavior that is enjoyable to observe.

Guiding children through their days of claiming themselves is not always easy and it is not always fun. Nevertheless, it is an essential part of a parent's opportunity to nurture and inspire that will result in confident actions and agreeable behaviors. For both the young child and the parents who shelter them, 'No' becomes a well-respected sign of strength and a welcome marker of healthy growth.

That is what all the foot stomping is about!

Olson Huff, MD

Olson's life has been one of many accomplishments as a father, a husband, and as one of America's most respected pediatricians. His significant contributions to the field of pediatrics has spanned over 35 years of clinical practice, teaching, medical administration, and program development.

Olson dedicated most of his career to focusing on children with special health care needs and the expansion of health care services to all children. He helped create a mobile dental program for underprivileged children in rural areas and developed the Olson Huff Center for Child Development as a model of interdisciplinary care for children with developmental disabilities of all kinds.

Olson has consulted to a number of children's foundations such as the Mission Healthcare Foundation and The Duke Endowment. In addition to those roles, he has served on a number of boards and commissions in North Carolina and nationally and was elected as president of the Board of the North Carolina Pediatric Society Foundation. He was also invited as Fellow to a number of institutes such as the Action for Children North Carolina. In this capacity, Olson focused on policy issues for health and safety of children. He is currently continuing his advocacy for children as chairman of the Committee on Federal Government Affairs of the American Academy of Pediatrics.

Olson serves as co-chairman of the Task Force on Obesity and Nutrition of the NC Health and Wellness Trust Fund Commission, which resulted in recommendations that have changed policies in North Carolina affecting activity and nutrition in public schools.

Olson's efforts have not gone unnoticed as he has been awarded a number of notable honors including the David Tayloe Senior award from the North Carolina Pediatric Society and the American Academy of Pediatrics Special Recognition Award for increasing access to dental health care for children.

The Lewis Hine Award from the National Child Labor Committee was also awarded to Olson in 2007 for his work to improve health care for low income children. Recognition of his contributions was also acknowledged when he was named one of the 100 most influential citizens of western North Carolina in the 20th century.

Olson's literary achievements include his self-penned book, *The Window of Childhood: Glimpses of Wonder and Courage*. Olson has also written extensively on issues relating to children's health and children with special health care needs, and serves as a member of the editorial board of the *North Carolina Medical Journal*.

Aggressive behavior

Some young children go through a stage of biting, hitting, and kicking. It can be frightening for parents, the victims, and for the child herself. Having a child with aggressive behavior can be a challenge for a parent. Monique, mom of three-year-old Jessica says:

‘I remember not wanting to go to playgroup when my child was going through a biting stage. I would hover over my daughter in fear that she would bite yet another child. The looks from some of the other parents were almost unbearable.’

Take a breath and remember, this is normal behavior. She may be doing these things to see the reaction it causes. Other reasons children bite, hit, or kick is that they become frustrated or angry and have not yet learned other ways to communicate.

What can I do about aggressive behavior?

- Become aware of any situations that may be a trigger for this behavior – sometimes it only happens while playing with a particular child, while playing with a certain toy, or even when the child is hungry or tired.
- Keep a close eye on your child while she is going through this stage. This is not a time for you to sit back and chat with the other parents. You will need to stay close so that you can head off the behavior before it happens. If you see your child becoming frustrated, you could try distracting her with another toy or activity, or help her to verbalize what she is trying to communicate. Give your child the needed words such as, ‘It’s my turn,’ or ‘I’m still using that.’ If you see she is

unable to control herself, remove her from the situation.

- As hard as it is, let other parents know about this potential aggressive behavior during play dates, and also advise your day care provider.
- Praise your child when she uses words instead of hitting and biting.
- If your child gets physical, stop the behavior immediately. Comfort the victim. Re-state the no hitting (or biting or kicking) rule and suggest alternative ways to behave, for example, 'Hitting hurts, it's not okay to hit. If you want the doll, you need to say to Rebecca, "Can I have a turn?"'
- Avoid reacting by humiliating or yelling at your child. This often makes the situation worse. Remember, your child is still learning appropriate ways to behave.

AGGRESSIVE BEHAVIOR – PARENT STORY

Nadia – two children aged seven and four

When my little boy turned four he really embraced 'boy things'. This was a bit of a double-edged sword – it was great that he was discovering what it means to be a boy, however it was like he went slightly overboard and became overly aggressive in his play. As he doesn't watch any violent TV or DVDs I realized that the aggressive play was coming from his interaction with other little boys who had been exposed to TV and DVDs depicting this type of behavior. I decided that we would talk about this type of play. I said while it might seem like fun you should never actually physically hit someone with a sword or weapon. I explained that it is pretend play and not real. I talked about how he would feel if someone came up to him being too rough and using a loud scary voice. He said that he would find it a bit scary. So I asked. 'Do you think it is something that you should be doing?' He said 'no'.

As it turned out, he really didn't like this type of play very much as it was scary. He joined in because he didn't know what else to do. We talked about saying to the boys in a firm voice that he doesn't want to play those games. We talked about alternative games to play such as being a construction worker in the sand pit or fireman rescuing people. Usually if my child is acting aggressive, there is a reason like this one behind it. I always look for the cause and make a plan from there. Since making this plan my boy hasn't been as aggressive in his play and he has a framework to use to help him think about what he'd rather be doing.

Angry feelings

For some young children, learning to deal with angry feelings can be a challenge. These feelings are new to them and they have not yet learned how to manage them. When children are angry they may hit, yell, throw, and say hurtful things such as 'I hate you' or 'You are the meanest mommy'. What can you do to help your child learn to manage his angry feelings?

- Stay cool. Getting angry yourself will usually make the problem worse. Talk in a quiet and calm manner.
- Acknowledge your child's anger: 'You feel so angry when Sammy takes your toys.' Sometimes just having the 'feeling' named lets the child know that someone understands and this may help to calm him down.
- Let your child know it is okay to be angry, but there are appropriate and inappropriate ways to express anger.
- If you feel your child is out of control, remove him from the situation. Wait until your child calms down before you try to talk to him. You may have to sit and hold him if he is intent on harming a sibling or others. You can say, 'I will let you go when you have calmed down.'
- If the child is old enough, talk with him to figure out what makes him feel angry. For example, is he being teased by siblings or other children at preschool? Is he feeling angry about a new baby?

- Teach your child to recognize he they feels angry. He may feel fear, a pain in the chest, or experience other signs such as clenched fists or rapid breathing.
- Think about how you manage your anger and model ways to deal with anger. For example, 'I'm feeling really angry at the moment, I think I need to count to ten and calm down a little.'

Show him positive ways to handle his angry feedings

- Ask him to draw a picture of his angry feelings.
- Have him tell someone when he is angry with them. Remind him to use his words. Give him the words if he does not have them yet. For example, 'Sam is feeling angry at you for knocking down his tower.'
- He can express angry feelings by tearing paper, punching a pillow, or by doing something physical like running, jumping, stamping feet, or going into another room to yell.
- Or he can blow up a paper bag and pop it.
- He can squeeze, punch, or pound playdough.

Some children pass through this stage rather quickly. For other children anger is part of their temperament, so it is important to learn how to manage these feelings. You know your child. If you are at all concerned with your child's behavior then talk to a family counselor.

ANGRY FEELINGS – PARENT STORY

Nadia – two children aged seven and four

My partner regularly travels and I have always prepared my children for this time of separation by role-playing what will happen, making simple books about where daddy goes and what he does there and that he comes back. We also make a paper chain for the number of days he is away and the children cut one off each morning. The time is marked by 'heart days' (I draw a heart on a few of the paper chains) and we do something special together. As time went by I became a little complacent about doing some of these activities. Now my son is four years old, and really connecting with the fact that he and daddy are both males and alike in many ways – he has become more attached and needs that male role around even more. He now gets quite angry when his dad leaves for the two-week-long business trips and I have to remember to make an extra big effort to help him explore his feelings about his dad leaving.

Now I am starting a week before his dad leaves and I tell him he is leaving and for how long and why he is leaving and when he will be back. He doesn't like me to talk about it because he says it makes him sad, however the feelings need to be dealt with otherwise he bottles them up and he becomes quite angry. I read him a simple book about daddy going away for work and how he packs his bags, flies on the airplane, does his work and then packs his bags and then flies home to him to get a big hug. The repetition and simplicity seems to help him understand what's happening and why it's happening. My son and I have talked about ways he can express his angry feelings about dad leaving and he came up with some pretty good ideas: stamp his feet when he feels angry, tell mommy when he is feeling angry so he can get extra cuddles, and bang on a tree with a stick to get the angry feelings out.

Doing all of these things has helped my son deal with his feelings about his dad leaving. We just need to remember these strategies and how important they are to both of our children.

Bathtime battles

Some young children develop a fear of the bath, others just don't see the point in getting clean. If your child is frightened of bath time, try to work out what is causing the fear. Is it the sound of the water going down the drain? Is it the depth of the water? Has she had a fall in the bath?

Here are some suggestions for encouraging your child to get in the bath:

- To encourage your child to get a good scrub in the tub let her have special toys that are only for bath time. They can be as simple as measuring cups, funnels, and spoons or one of the many bath toys available in stores. Put in only a few toys at a time and rotate them regularly.
- Think about the toys your child already has that may be good for bath play. Samantha, mom of four-year-old Grace says, 'When my daughter was three (and hated washing her hair) she had so many toy ponies that we kept a couple for bath time – the thought of washing their manes and tail would entice her into the bath for a hair wash.'
- Get in with your child – she is less likely to resist if you are in the bath too!
- If your child is not too dirty, skip bath time for a night and just wipe her face and hands.
- Experiment with water levels. Some children are more comfortable with only a little water in the bath. (Remember to only fill the bath up to the waist of your smallest child.)
- Try different times of the day. If your child is tired at the end of the day and you think this is contributing to the bath refusal, change bath time

to another time in the day, such as before or after naptime.

- Change the scenery. Janet says, 'When my son went through a stage of hating bath time, we tried washing him in the laundry sink and he loved it.'
- Take your child out of the bath before you empty it if you feel the sound of the water going down the drain is part of the problem.
- A few drops of food coloring used occasionally works wonders for getting a reluctant child into the bath.
- Remember that while your child is playing in the bath she is learning. Wonderful math and science concepts can be explored, such as measuring, estimating, sinking, and floating.
- Allow plenty of time for playing, but if she doesn't want to linger then get her out after a quick wash.
- Incorporate bath time into the bedtime routine. Children thrive on routines and like to know when things are going to happen. For example, if bath time always comes after dinner and is followed by stories, your child will learn what happens next and will be less likely to resist.
- Play music, sing songs, or tell stories while she's in the tub. This added incentive encourages many

children to enjoy this time of their day.
- Lastly, if you are the parent who works during the day then this is a wonderful opportunity to interact with your child. Play, have fun, and don't forget she is only little for a short time.

Always make sure you supervise your child while in the bath.

BATHTIME BATTLES – PARENT STORY

Ted and Michelle – twins aged two and a half

One of our daughters developed a fear of bath time around the age of two. This developed after a fall in the bath that resulted in her face becoming submerged (which she hates). She would cling to us when we tried to put her in the tub with her sister, and if we forced the issue she would cry until we took her out. After weeks of dreading bath time we changed tactics. Instead of having a bath at the end of the day, we changed bath time to the morning, after breakfast. I dressed the girls in their bathing suits and filled the tub with a couple of inches of water. I had bought some new bath toys, which I placed in the tub. I showed the girls the new toys and asked them if they wanted to play with the water toys (I didn't mention bath time or washing). They both happily climbed in and spent 30 minutes playing in the tub. I did this for a week gradually increasing the amount of water. We then changed to evening 'water play' so we could show daddy. Eventually the bathing suits came off and we are back to pleasant bath times!

Hair washing refusal

What can we do? Many young children love to take a bath but protest loudly when it's time to wash their hair. Here are a couple of ideas to make washing hair easier:

- Make sure you use a shampoo of the 'no tears' variety.
- Have your child hold a rolled-up washcloth over his eyes.
- Put some interesting pictures on the ceiling to encourage him to look up for easy rinsing.
- Try using a squeeze bottle filled with water to rinse hair if he is reluctant to lie down.
- He may feel more comfortable with having his hair rinsed by a hand-held shower attachment.
- Use a purpose-made rinse guard to protect his face.
- Let him wash your hair first and make it seem like fun!
- Put a doll with hair (waterproof, of course) in the bath and let him play at washing hair.

- Sing a hair washing song such as 'This is the way we wash your hair'. Tell him hair washing will be over when the song is over.
- Unless he is getting very dirty, don't worry about washing hair every day. He may only need a hair wash once a week.

HAIR WASHING REFUSAL – PARENT STORY

Antonija – five children aged seven, five, three, two, and six weeks

My three-year-old son would not let me wash his hair, he would get very upset and I would be rather stressed. I asked my husband to shower with him to see if he would let his dad wash his hair. He happily let his father shampoo and condition his hair without one tear and without getting upset. I think he enjoyed spending one-on-one time with his dad. After a few weeks of doing this, my son now lets me wash his hair without a second thought.

My two-year-old daughter didn't like getting her hair washed either, until I accidentally made it fun for her. I filled a jug to rinse the shampoo off her and she ducked her head at the last moment. The water made her hair hang down in front of her face and looked like a waterfall. She likes it so much that she asks me to do it again and again, long after the shampoo has been rinsed out.

Chores

There are many ways young children can help around the house; even two year olds can learn to put away their own pajamas. Involving children in family chores helps to develop a sense of cooperation and teamwork in a family. Children who grow in responsibility also grow in self-esteem (a prerequisite for achievement in the real world). Whenever possible, turn work into fun. Responsible kids feel good about themselves. The best way to keep a household running smoothly is to ensure everyone in the house knows what is expected of them. By including your child in this shared sense of responsibility, you are instilling the values of family unity and teamwork within your child.

It is extremely important that the chores you select for your child should be developmentally appropriate. As a parent, find ways to incorporate responsibility into your child's life – encourage him to see tasks through to the end.

First of all:

- Assess your child's skill level – what is he capable of doing?
- Only assign developmentally appropriate tasks for your child to complete, otherwise you will be automatically setting him up for failure.
- Sit down and make a list of chores that need to be done. Encourage your child to think of things around the house that he thinks he can

do. This will give your child a sense of control. He is also more likely to stick with a chore that he volunteered for, or particularly enjoys doing.

Getting started:

- Do not overwhelm your child with too many chores. It can be very daunting, especially if she is getting this kind of responsibility for the first time.
- Personally demonstrate what you want her to do for every new task or chore. Show her exactly what is to be done, and how, and try to make it fun. Take turns at choosing 'chore music'.
- Set a time limit that is developmentally appropriate, such as sweeping leaves for five minutes and using a timer. Supervise her until she has mastered it.

Ongoing:

- If possible, establish a routine for your child to follow for completing his chores. By doing the same chores at the same time every day, your child will be less likely to forget them.
- Post a list of your child's chores and responsibilities where he can see it every day. For a younger child, draw pictures so she can easily see what she needs to do. She may like to check it

off each day. Children often love the satisfaction of placing completed stickers on their chore chart.

- Reward your child for completing her chores. Hugs, kisses, verbal praise, and having a friend over are all great rewards. Children enjoy hearing that they are doing a good job just as much as adults do, so make a point of saying something positive about your child's progress each day.
- Some families pay their children for completing chores, others feel payment is not necessary as they are contributing to the daily life of a family home.

Chores are a great way for children to learn responsibility. Contributing to family life may be a source of earned pride and self-esteem. The trick is ensuring the chores assigned to your child don't create a sense of tension, arguments, and ultimately frustration. Let's be honest, few kids (or adults) like to do chores, but teaching children responsibility not only helps you with the task of keeping a house in good shape, but also enhances a child's self-esteem as he begins to view himself as an essential part of the family and household.

What are some areas of responsibility you could give your child?

- Keeping his room tidy, such as making his bed, keeping his toys tidy, putting his clothes away.

- Morning organization – getting dressed, getting his backpack ready, putting on his shoes.
- Helping with meal times, such as setting the table, emptying the dishwasher, helping with food preparation.
- Household cleaning, such as dusting, cleaning windows, sweeping, vacuuming.
- General duties like feeding pets, watering plants, getting the mail.

Have a family brainstorm of what needs to be done and ask for volunteers.

CHORES – PARENT STORIES

Bess – two children aged six and four

We tried to get our children doing chores. It was a nightmare and didn't work at all. The dog starved and short-term memory issues meant I spent huge amounts of time re-explaining the chores on a daily basis. We then decided to give them some super simple chores, like put your toys away and get a sticker on the reward chart. Real chores sort of started around five years of age and have improved each year since. They still have motivation issues. We don't pay them in money but they do get 'rewards' like new books and clothes. (Truth is I'd still buy them the books and clothes but they don't know that!)

Lily – three children aged seven, five, and three

We have a whiteboard with all the expectations clearly drawn or written on for our children. Mornings are chaos in our home, so they have lists of what to do and they know why they are doing them. We don't pay our kids for chores; they are part of the family and are responsible for doing small tasks that help our home run smoothly. We do make chores fun, we play a lot of loud music when cleaning. We try to do a big cleaning session on Saturday mornings followed by a shared lunch. I write the jobs for each family member on toilet tissue and hand out the sections, the kids love it. When their list is complete, they flush it down the toilet!

Defiance – When your child says 'No!'

One of the most common complaints parents have is when they have asked their child to do something and the child says 'No!' Even when a child doesn't say no, she will often ignore the request and carry on with what she is doing. This is normal behavior and your child will require some convincing to see things your way! Try the following strategies next time your child shows defiant behavior:

- Be clear and consistent about your expectations. Communicate clearly, get her attention and make eye contact. Make your request short and positive. Try not to nag.
- Practice what you preach! Ensure you are modeling the behavior you expect from your child. Are you constantly yelling out 'No!' when asked to do things? Think about your behavior (and your partner's), as your child will be watching and learning from your example.
- Phrase your requests. Think about how you are asking your child to do things. For example, are you saying, 'It's time to get in the bath,' as opposed to, 'Would you like to get in the bath now?' Sometimes something as simple as how you phrase things can stop 'No!' being a possible answer.
- Be patient. Let your child know you are on her side. Try not to rush her, be understanding, and try not to get angry.
- Set realistic goals. Children need limits placed on them. It makes them feel safe and you will need to be consistent and realistic with your expectations. They have the right to say 'no' if what you are asking is unreasonable. Think about your child's age and what she is physically, mentally, and emotionally capable of doing.

- Have as few rules as possible but stick to them. Sit down as a family and talk about what rules are important and what are the consequences if they are not followed.
- Give warnings. Negative behavior may be avoided if children know what is happening next. If you are at the playground and you have had difficulties in the past getting your child to come home, try giving the five minute warning. Say, 'We are going in five minutes,' and have your child acknowledge that she has heard you. Of course, it is important to then leave in five minutes, or your child will not believe you next time.
- Reward good behavior. Catch your child being good. Reward her with positive reinforcement and plenty of hugs!
- Stay positive. Imagine there is a video camera following you through your day. If you played it back and counted how many positive comments, as opposed to negative comments you said to your child, how would you do?
- Time out. Your child may need to go to a safe time out space to think about her behavior. Some parents chose to send their child to her room to cool down. Make sure you clearly state why you have put your child in time out and what

behavior you are expecting. Time out does not need to be viewed as a negative place; it can be a calm quiet place to go. You may need to put yourself there from time to time!

- Empower your child. Give her opportunities to make her own choices. A choice of two things is plenty. Try saying, 'It's time for a wash – would you like a bath or a shower tonight?'
- Choose your battles. Some things are simply not worth battling about. Think about your child's behavior and decide if there are some things you are prepared to let slide, such as your child's terrible color combinations in her clothing choices.
- Distract, distract, distract. Always try to avoid situations that are going to cause problems (where possible), but if you find yourself in one of those situations use distraction to avoid a scene.

We need to remember that disciplining our children does not have to mean controlling them. It means teaching them ways to control themselves. Punishment might get them to behave, but only because they are afraid of the consequences. The best thing for your child is to be intrinsically motivated – that is to do the right thing because they want to, because it makes the day more fun and makes them feel good.

In conclusion, be patient and consistent with your approach. Remember your child is a little person who is growing and evolving into an individual. Have respect for the learning she is doing but ensure she is safe and happy at the same time!

DEFIANCE – PARENT STORY

Chantelle and Taj – four children aged eleven, nine, six, and three

We both find dealing with defiance difficult. It is hard not to get angry and react when your child tells you 'No!' We have four children, so we have had plenty of experience with this. We have learned that if we react with anger to our children's defiance it only makes matters worse. This doesn't mean that we accept defiant behavior (we are both quite strict), but we take a breath and deal with it as calmly as possible. We use consequences, distraction, and we try to remember to notice cooperative behavior – our children work out fairly quickly it is not worth their while to be defiant. Our three year old is challenging us with this now, and even though we think 'Here we go again,' we feel confident that with consistency on our part he will work it out.

Dressing challenges

Oh the joys of morning madness. The key to smooth mornings is *organization*. Getting a non-compliant four year old to get dressed can sometimes be a challenge. Young children are egocentric and unpredictable, which can make them very hard to live with at times. Here are some strategies for you to try:

- Stay calm and try to not make a big deal of getting dressed. A sense of humor can also be helpful.
- Have him get dressed as soon as he gets up and not right before you want to leave.
- Choose clothes the night before. Have your child choose which clothes he wants to wear, and then there is no further discussion on the matter (unless there is a weather surprise).
- If your child insists on wearing the same clothes, consider buying more sets of the same clothing perhaps with different colors. He will eventually become bored with the 'uniform' he has restricted himself to wearing.
- When getting dressed, distract him with a story or talk about the events planned for the day. Sing a getting dressed song. Have a getting dressed race.
- Ask for your child's help to get him dressed (reverse psychology sometimes works).

- Try using reward charts and lots of positive reinforcement.
- If he refuses to get dressed, consider taking him out in his pajamas. Pack clothing to take with you.

DRESSING CHALLENGES – PARENT STORIES

Catherine – one child aged four

My four year old used to make my mornings a living hell. I was so stressed and angry, I felt like I was bribing him constantly and nothing would happen without the promise of a treat. Mornings left me feeling like a parenting failure. A friend suggested I let my child go to sleep in the clothes he wanted to wear in the morning. I thought it was ridiculous, but I tried it and it was great. Eventually he started asking to dress himself in the mornings, but it helped us get through a tough time. Talk to other parents, we all have our challenges!

Crystal – three children aged seven, four, and one

My son had major issues with getting dressed in the morning. As a family, we started having fun 'dressing' games on the weekend. We would put a set of clothes at one end of the room and each family member would take turns hopping or crawling down the room in a relay and putting on the dress-up clothes and running back. We played it in teams and as individuals and I think it made 'getting dressed' a fun thing to do. In the end, I think the games, plus a star chart and leaving him to do it without me fussing over him helped. Looking back on it, I can't believe it was such a major issue for me, he is older now and we have *new* issues to contend with.

Getting children to sleep in their own bed

Some parents enjoy co-sleeping with their children, or don't mind if they have a night visitor. If this works in your family, stick with it. Others would like to sleep 'kid-free'. If you would like your child to sleep in her own bed, check out the suggestions below:

- Create a consistent bedtime routine (see Chapter Three), that is enjoyable and calming for your child.
- Put your child to sleep in her own bed. It is confusing for her if you let her fall asleep in your bed or somewhere else, then move her.
- Tell your child, 'It's time to sleep in your bed. I'll see you in the morning.' Give her a hug and a kiss then leave the room.
- If your child follows you, take her gently by the hand and lead her back to bed. Do this every time your child follows you. Stay calm and try to give your child as little attention as possible.

- If your child cries, sit beside the bed for a few minutes. You might try patting her gently or lying by her until she is calm and sleepy enough for you to leave.
- The goal is for your child to be able to fall asleep on her own, in her own bed. If she becomes used to sleeping in your bed, or in her bed with you beside her, then this is what she will expect every night. If she wakes in the night and she is used to having you next to her to fall asleep, then this is what she will need to get back to sleep.
- If you are consistent, your child should be falling asleep in her own bed within a few days to a week.
- If your child continues to get out of her bed, then you need to try and think why this is happening. Is she getting enough time with you? Does she have any fears? Is she just not tired at the time you are trying to put her to bed? Talk to your child or try to read some children's books to her that deal with these issues.
- If your child climbs into your bed after you've gone to sleep, get up at once and take her back to her own bed. This is hard to do when you're sleepy, but it is important to do. The faster you get up the better the chance your child will settle back into her bed. Sit with her for a few minutes

until she settles back.

- Remember, it's easier to keep your child out of your bed if you do not start the practice in the first place.
- If you enjoy co-sleeping, go ahead and do what works best for you and your family. Some families like to compromise by putting the child on a mattress on the floor by their bed.

GETTING CHILDREN TO SLEEP IN THEIR OWN BED – PARENT STORY

Nadia – two children aged seven and four

This can be such a tricky one. Between bad dreams, scary shadows in bedrooms, and loud thunderstorms, sleep is prone to all sorts of potential problems. Both my children have had hiccups in their sleeping patterns and I have found that the most successful thing to do is to be consistent. They have a well-established routine in which they fall asleep in their own bed. This makes it easier to return them to their own bed if they wake up during the night. If one of my children comes in late at night, I give them a cuddle in my bed and then carry them back to their own bed. To settle them down, I sing the same songs that I always sing to them at bedtime. I ask them if they want me to stay until they get back to sleep. Sometimes they want me to and sometimes they don't, but I like to give them the option. If they do want me to stay, I usually sit quietly beside their bed or lie at the end of the bed if I'm really tired. Once they are settled and back to sleep, I slip back into my own bed. My little boy went through a stage of waking at around 2 am, and I had to stay with him until he fell asleep – this lasted for several weeks. I was worried that he'd gotten himself into a pattern and would never stop. However, after a couple of weeks he began sleeping through the night again and hasn't had a problem since. So, I think being gentle and loving is a good way to go.

Giving up a bottle

Some children are very attached to their bottles, but there are many good reasons for transitioning to a cup. Prolonged bottle usage can cause problems, including tooth decay and ear infection, a lack of interest in eating (by filling up on milk and juice), and weight problems – drinking too many bottles a day is an easy way for children to take in unneeded extra calories.

Many experts suggest starting to wean off the bottle at twelve months, because children over the age of one are more resistant to change. But, in the reality of life, this sometimes does not happen – without your meaning to, you suddenly have a two, three or even four year old still drinking from a bottle. For some parents this is fine, but if you would like to help your child move onto a cup try the following suggestions.

Usually, the night-time bottle is the most challenging one to wean but it can be done. With persistence and some of the strategies listed below you will have success:

- There are times you should avoid bottle weaning – for example, arrival of a new baby, moving to a new house, or any other major changes.
- The first thing you could try is simply switching your child's bottle for a cup. Hand your child the cup without making a big deal and see what he does. He might be interested in it and want to try it. Alternatively, they might completely refuse it. If this happens, don't push the issue. Simply give him a bottle and try again a few days later.
- If you decide you would like your child to give up his bottle, go shopping with your child and let him pick out a sippy cup. Sometimes having control over the change is enough for children to wean themselves.
- In the transition phase, you could try offering him the cup filled with his favorite drink after he has had a meal. Be careful about offering lots of juice. It might seem like a great way to transition from the bottle to the sippy cup, but it can also create a new habit you will need to break. Make sure your child gets plenty of water and the appropriate servings of milk each day for his age and occasionally offer juice. Children aged two to four

years old need five servings of milk, yogurt, or cheese a day. Remember one serving of milk is half a cup. That means that a 9 ounce bottle of milk has more than two serves.

- Over a gradual period of time (dependent on your child's willingness), gradually replace his morning and night-time bottle with a cup. Usually the night bottle is the last one to go.
- Many people try offering diluted milk in the bottle and undiluted milk in the cup, while others try offering an unappealing drink in the bottle such as grapefruit juice, making the milk in the cup seem more attractive.
- If your child wakes in the night, try offering him a sip of water from his sippy cup.
- Be honest with your child and explain to him that it is time to give the bottle away and why. It can be a tough habit to break; buying a new soft toy or another treat may help.
- If your child has friends who are drinking from cups, it would be a good idea to do some socializing with them. Have a party or play date where snacks are served and make a big deal out of some special cups that you have provided for the event.
- Many parents worry that their child will not drink enough if he doesn't have a bottle. Be

inventive, use lots of different types of cups, tumblers, different plastic containers, crushed ice and so on to tempt your child to drink.

- Try to be positive with your child – don't ridicule him. Remind him how well he is doing and praise him when he asks for or uses a cup.
- Usually the most emotionally charged bottle time is bedtime. You will need to create a special bedtime routine that is not centered on drinking. Start with a quiet game, then bath time, story time, and maybe some quiet talking time in which you ask him about his day. Involve your child in your routine. Tuck your child in bed and tell him a story about your childhood. Tell him about your favorite toy, bike and so on. Make the bedtime routine a time for sharing and not a time for drinking. Make sure you end up with him in bed, so that when he is sleepy, you can kiss him goodnight.
- If your child wants to go back to a bottle, try distracting him and make sure you give him lots of extra hugs and attention.

Remember that this process takes time and patience, both on your part and on your child's. Try to be calm and positive while your child is learning something new. It will help the process go smoother and everyone will be a lot happier.

Remember, never put your child to bed with a bottle as it can cause ear infections and tooth decay.

GIVING UP A BOTTLE – PARENT STORY

Ted and Michelle – twins aged two and a half

We didn't mean for our children to keep using a bottle after age one, but it was the easiest way for us to get the two of them off to sleep at the same time, especially if Ted was working late. We took the girls to the dentist when they were two and when the dentist explained that this was not a good idea for their teeth, we decided to get rid of the bottles. We chose a time when I knew Ted would not be working late for a few days, so we could work together. We decided to use the cold turkey method. A couple of days before, we talked to the girls about not needing a bottle anymore as they were 'big girls', and we took them shopping for a new soft toy to sleep with. On the day we were going cold turkey, we wrapped the bottles up and 'mailed' them to a new baby. At bedtime they both asked for their bottles. We reminded them that the bottles were with a new baby now and we gave the girls their soft toys. They both had a little cry, but settled down much quicker than I thought they would. I was actually quite nervous about the whole thing. After a week they were both fine with it.

Giving up a pacifier

Often people are amazed that parents let their children use pacifiers for so long. But, if you are the parent of a child addicted to her pacifier, you will know the peace that comes from its use and the battles that occur when you suggest it needs to go! Many parents accept its use until the first birthday, with a vast majority trying to wean their child off her pacifier by the second birthday.

First off, decide when the time is right. Ensure there are no major changes or stresses occurring in your child's life. Decide if you are going to go 'cold-turkey' or 'slowly but surely'.

Here are some strategies that you can try:

- Try offering to exchange something to replace the pacifier: for example, a family outing or a new toy.
- Avoid getting angry with your child or throwing the pacifier in the trash (unless your child agrees).
- Many parents try cutting a small hole in the pacifier. The child thinks it is 'broken' and often simply stops using it. (Never leave your child alone with the pacifier if you do this.)
- Arrange a visit from the Binkie Fairy. She comes and collects pacifiers (often from outside your front door overnight) and gives them to new

babies who need them. In exchange, she often leaves a little treat.

- Some children will accept having the pacifier mailed to a 'little baby'.
- Enlist your dentist's assistance. Prior to your child's dental appointment, contact the dentist and ask him to talk to your child about pacifiers and teeth development. Often hearing the suggestion from an 'authority' can encourage a child to give up the habit.
- You could try a slower method of weaning her off her pacifier. Set some rules for pacifier use, such as allowing her to use it in the car, stroller, and bedroom. Then only use it for naps and at bedtime. Make bedtime the last one to go. You may have some rough nights but stick to your decision and try to be as positive as possible with your child.
- Some parents use a product which helps children to stop sucking their thumb. Coat the pacifier with the bitter-tasting liquid.
- If you are trying the cold-turkey method, try doing it on a quiet weekend when nothing is planned. You may have a lot of tears and broken sleep, so be prepared for the worst, or you may be pleasantly surprised!
- Keep your sense of humor. All children give up their pacifiers sooner or later. Good luck!

Marnie – three children aged nine, six, and four

My three-year-old son used to *love* his pacifier. He learned to speak with it in his mouth, walked around with a spare one in his hand, and had others hidden in various places around the house. He is my youngest child and my other two children gave up their pacifiers when they were two. One day we saw a toy advertised on the television and he said he wanted it. I said I would buy it for him if he stopped using his pacifier *today*! I thought there was no way he'd do it, *but he did*! He gathered them up from around the house and we ceremoniously put them out in the trash can. That night we had tears and he asked if he could get one from the trash but I cuddled him and told him stories and the trash can was never visited. He was obviously ready.

Melissa and Ben – one child aged five

I let my daughter use her pacifier until she was four. We restricted its use, but she loved it and it wasn't a problem for me. She could only use it on her bed. It wasn't allowed to be used anywhere else. When she started kindergarten, she simply stopped using it because of the social pressures.

Judy – three children aged six, three, and two

Our first child used a pacifier up to the age of two. I didn't particularly want him to, but I guess I slipped into giving it to him to help him go to sleep, and eventually he couldn't go to sleep without it. Then I started to give it to him when he was unsettled, and before you know it, it became like an appendage, that I dared not leave the house without. As he got older and began to crawl, then walk, the issue of hygiene reared its head, as it was often dropped then quickly put back into his mouth.

Around eighteen months we started saying that the pacifier needed to stay in bed. We made it a routine that when he woke he would place the pacifier in a special box next to the bed. It took a while to get this routine going, but with persistence it prevailed.

At two we 'lost' the pacifier and replaced it with a small toy that he sleeps with instead of the pacifier. This toy is also placed in the box when he wakes. The transition from pacifier to toy took about four days.

Unfortunately, we didn't learn from the first child and reintroduced the pacifier with the next two children ... such is life!

Lying

Living with a young child can be entertaining and challenging. Take for example the four year old who is standing by a puddle of milk and is looking you in the eye and saying, 'I didn't spill the milk.' Hmmmm? Often the challenge is working out how to react. All children will lie occasionally and although lying is a normal part of a child's development, it is not something you can overlook. It is a parent's job to teach children honesty.

Not all lying is dishonest. There is a big difference between being dishonest – lying or cheating – and 'making things up', as young children often do when engaged in fantasy play. If we teach children that not telling the truth is 'a bad thing', some young children might assume that it is also a bad thing to pretend to be a princess or an astronaut. Although you should discourage your child from deliberately lying and cheating, you should let him know that it is fine to role-play and pretend.

All parents want to raise honest children. At around the age of three, four, or five, children begin to experiment with lying and cheating. They do this because they are learning about honesty and the differences between what is right and wrong. Because parents are their child's first and best teacher, children learn how to behave from them. If your child has just begun testing you by lying, remember she is experimenting. Let her know it is wrong and explain why. She will not learn immediately and will need gentle and continuous guidance from you.

Here are some tips to help you deal with lying:

- Often we put our children in situations where they feel they have to lie. Try to avoid saying, 'Did you draw on the wall?' Instead state, 'We have a rule in our home that we only color on paper. Let's get some towels and water and clean this up now.' Your child did something wrong, she realizes she did something wrong, but for obvious reasons she does not want to admit it and be punished. Put yourself in her place and work out where you draw the line.
- When your child tells a lie, use it as an opportunity to talk about why being truthful is so important. Calling her a liar or yelling may cause your child to keep lying to avoid blame.
- To encourage truth telling, try removing the consequences. Say, 'No matter what you did, I promise I won't get angry so long as you tell the truth.' Many kids lie because they know they have done something wrong and they want to avoid your punishment or disappointment. Focus on what you want your child to learn: being honest. When your child tells the truth about something she has done wrong, be sure to praise her.
- Practice what you preach. Try to avoid those little white lies for which we adults are famous. If you say, 'Thank you, I love oatmeal cookies,' to

someone who gives you a gift and your child knows you dislike oatmeal cookies, make sure you explain why you said it. Sometimes we do make our lives somewhat complicated!

- Try not to share your child's 'cute stories' with adults for comedy purposes. At least not in front of your child, as this can often reinforce that lying is okay and is in fact funny and cute.
- Tell the story about 'The Boy Who Cried Wolf'. Talk about why it is important to tell the truth. Discuss the issue of trust with your child. Explain why it is hard for us to trust and believe someone who tells many lies.
- Encourage your child to have an imagination. Just ensure she understands the difference between fantasy and reality.

Developing morals and values takes time, but these are usually well established by the time a child reaches the age of ten. Remember all young children go through this stage, so be patient and consistent.

LYING – PARENT STORY

> **Matthew – three children aged eight, four, and eighteen months**
>
> My four year old is a good kid and he tries hard to always do the right thing. If he ever does something that

> he knows is wrong (which is rare), he hates the thought of disappointing me. He will lie about it and deny that he was responsible. For example, he and the neighbors' children recently took part in eating the candy put aside for trick-or-treaters. When I found out, he became very upset and tried to tell me it was the other two and not him. This was not true as one of our other neighbors saw all three of them. I waited until he had calmed down and explained to him that if you do something wrong it is best to face up to it. I told him everyone makes mistakes and I would always love him no matter what he did. We talked about how he would feel if the other children had been punished and he hadn't. This is something we will continue to work on and hopefully he will feel able to tell me the truth in the future.

Picky eaters

The eating habits of this age group are often frustrating and mysterious. At times, they seem to survive on less food than a bird requires, and at others, they appear to be an eating machine, consuming everything in sight. Sometimes they claim something is wrong with the food, such as one thing on their plate is touching another! Young children often resist new foods, not because they are being difficult but because of their sensitivity to textures, smells, and tastes.

Here are some tips to help you help your picky eater:

- Many young children appear to live off air. If you actually watch what your child eats throughout an entire day, you might be surprised. Often young children are 'grazers'. They eat little bits of this and that throughout the day. As they are *so* active, it's probably a good way for them to eat at this age. If they graze throughout the day, they are constantly refuelling their active bodies.
- Keep a written or mental journal of what your child is eating during the day. With this information, you'll really be able to get an idea of how much food is eaten and when the eating is happening. You may be surprised at how much he actually does eat.
- The trick with children who graze is to make sure you have plenty of healthy grazing food available. Melissa suggests, 'I make up a healthy snacking lunch box for each child and keep it sitting in the refrigerator. They take what they want, when they feel they need it. The only rule we have is no snacking after 3.30 pm.'
- Avoid giving your young child lots of processed snacks. He'll fill up on empty calories and will have trouble getting all the nutritional needs met during the day.

- Serve lunch and dinner on a plate that has a nice variety of food on it. The main meal can be incorporated as well, but just pop on a few raw chopped vegetables with a yummy healthy dip. Have your child mix the dip with you and place the veggies on the plate in a fun pattern or make a funny face out of them. The point is to make the healthy food fun!
- Some children do not like the taste of cooked vegetables. Serve a variety of raw vegetables and see which ones your child likes. If all else fails you can try to puree some vegetables and include them in spaghetti sauces and casseroles. You can also make muffins with vegetables in them.
- Try growing a few vegetables in your own garden. I have seen many 'non-vegetable eaters' consume loads of the 'dreaded green stuff' when they have grown and picked it themselves.
- Don't draw meal times out and make them a struggle. You want your child to feel positive about healthy foods.
- A child needs to be exposed to a food at least ten times before he becomes used to the taste and texture of it. So be patient and keep offering small servings of new foods in as many ways as you can.
- Try to respect your child's food dislikes and don't insist that he be a member of 'the clean plate club'.

- Serving small portions will help. Children burn up many calories quickly and they have smaller stomachs.
- Remember, children can be very demanding about wanting certain foods, especially sweets. Reserve these for treat time only and don't become a hostage to food demands. For a 'sweet treat' give fruits (peaches, strawberries, apples, grapes) and non-fat dairy products like yogurt. These are nutritious complements to a healthy diet and often turn 'picky eaters' into real gourmets!

PICKY EATERS – PARENT STORY

Melissa and Dave – two children aged four and two

Sally was a great eater as a baby – we used to call her the baby bird because she would open her mouth and the food would go in. When she was around two years old, she would eat during breakfast and lunch, but when it came to dinner, hardly any food was going in. Meal times where going on forever! The whole thing became ridiculous, with me performing all kinds of tricks to get her to eat. I realized I needed to change my expectations. I gave her a smaller plate and put much less food on it – this seemed to help her to think that what she was eating was achievable. I also had her help me prepare some meals so she could choose how many of certain foods would go on her plate. I changed my expectation on the variety of foods I expected her to eat – I had her try really small amounts of foods she didn't like and after a while she did develop a taste for a bigger variety of foods. I was dubious about the letting her try it at least ten times rule, but it really does work! She now eats a variety of foods – I still get a kick out of her saying, and 'This dinner looks yummy.'

Shopping

Shopping with young children is not for the faint-hearted. Some parents have the luxury of getting time to do grocery shopping without their children. If you are not one of these parents and you do need to take the children with you, here are some suggestions for making it a more pleasant experience:

- Avoid shopping if your young children are tired and hungry. In fact, try to avoid shopping if *you* are tired and hungry.
- If it is available and you like the idea, use internet shopping and have your groceries delivered.
- Create a list and be organized so that you are not in the store any longer than you need to be.
- Give yourself enough time. Children feel stressed when they are rushed, and this is when the

behavior starts to go downhill. Tash writes, 'I used to try to rush up and down the aisle with my two year old trying to break the shopping world record. One day I asked myself, "What are you doing?" *Chill!* I decided to slow down. If that meant letting her having a "turn" at pushing the cart, or stopping to look at the doggies and kitties on the packets in the pet food aisle, then that is what we did. We were both less stressed and happier at the end.'

- Let them play. Okay, I can hear you thinking, 'What is he talking about?' What I mean is, children are more likely to be cooperative if what they are doing is fun. Tash says, 'I remember spending one whole shopping trip with my two-year-old daughter and her friend crawling behind the cart as cats. As long as I stayed in character ('Here kitties'), they would do whatever I wanted.'
- Shopping is filled with great learning opportunities. Try these phrases out: 'Could you get the yellow packet, please?' or 'See the one that starts with B? or 'We need the square box.'
- Tell your children ahead of time what type of behavior you expect. Children cannot read your mind. Spell it out for them. Do you want your children to take turns at putting items in the cart? Do they need to stay by you? Let them know.

- If you are taking snacks and drinks, let them know. Explain that if they are hungry or thirsty they will be having the food and drink that you brought with you. Letting them know before you leave that you will not be purchasing treats may help to avoid a later tantrum.
- Involve your children in shopping by helping to look for certain items, placing items in the cart, and crossing off items from the list. Children love to help. This tip can also help the fussy eater. If a child has helped to choose a food, then she is more likely to eat it.
- Take snacks and drinks to avoid the inevitable hunger pangs at the sight of all that food. Tash explains, 'I always took snacks for my daughter when we went shopping because I never wanted her to get into the habit of expecting something every time we went to the store. I do now occasionally get her a treat, but she doesn't expect one every time.'
- To keep your children safe, stay with them at all times. Keep them seated when in the cart if they are young enough, and use the restraint.
- Visit the toilet or do diaper changes before you get into the store. We all know this does not always work, so if your little one needs a change or to go to the toilet, then just leave the cart near

a checkout, and tell a staff member you will be back. Don't get angry – as the saying goes, 'When you've got to go, you've got to go.' This happens to the best of us.

- Remember to praise your child for good behavior. For example, 'I really like the way you are staying close to the cart today.'

SHOPPING – PARENT STORY

Jane and Mikel – four children aged six, four, two, and ten months

I am now a mom of four small children, roughly two years apart in ages, the youngest being almost ten months. I have always shopped with my children, never having the luxury of leaving them with grandparents. I also believed that they would get used to going to the store.

Here are my tips:

- I always went when the baby had had a feed.
- I would only go when I was sure the children were happy and not tired or hungry.
- I always take snacks with me for the children to eat while I am grocery shopping (a little bag of raisins or dates or a piece of fruit).
- If I knew it was going to be a long shop, then I would have the bit of food that took the longest to eat for the neediest part of my shopping trip.

- When my two eldest were too big for the cart, I would give them an activity. I would tell them, 'Skip to the end and then jump back to me,' as I went up and down each supermarket aisle.
- Similarly, if we had a lengthy wait in the checkout line, I would have them skip and touch something far away and then hop back to me or run and touch a certain color – anything to keep them amused as I shopped.
- There have been many times when shopping has been a nightmare for me, and it has usually been when I have taken tired kids.
- I don't take them clothes shopping because that is not interesting for them.
- I always tell them how wonderful they are when I take them shopping, and how I love taking them. This makes them try to be just as good the next time.

Sibling rivalry

Do your children fight? Is it driving you nuts? Sibling rivalry is common and very normal. It can be very distressing and exhausting for parents. Believe it or not, sibling rivalry does have benefits for your children. Disagreements with one another teach children how to resolve differences, learn problem-solving skills, and that there are acceptable and unacceptable ways to express themselves. Parents can help decrease the amount of sibling rivalry by spending time alone with each child, by avoiding comparing children, and by teaching children positive ways to express feelings. Here are some ways to help your children live with each other:

- Teach them that it's okay to feel angry but it's not okay to be physically angry and hurt others. Angry feelings are normal (see Angry Feelings on page 80) and children need to learn how to express them with their words. Teach them to say to their siblings, 'I feel angry when you take my toy away from me.'
- If children are physically fighting, separate the children until they calm down. When they have settled down have your children sit with each other and help them to work it out. If you feel they are able to, have them say what they will do differently next time.
- Do not assume the child doing the hitting is at fault. Children are masters at pushing each other's buttons. Be aware of what might have gone on beforehand. Although it is never okay to hit, the 'victim' may have been teasing the 'hitter' for many hours.
- If the children are bickering, try to remain calm and stay out of your children's argument. Ignore the arguing if you can. Leave the room or have them continue their argument away from

you. Often children can settle their own arguments, which is a great skill for them to learn.

- If the arguing is too loud or rough to ignore, separate the children for 30 to 60 minutes. You might say, 'Since you can't play without fighting, you both have to play by yourselves.' Then send each child to a different part of the house. No TV or computer is allowed during this time as this is rewarding behavior you want to change. After a break from each other, they will hopefully be better playmates.
- Most of the time it is best to not try to find out who started the fight since this means parents have to decide who is the 'good guy' and who is the 'bad guy'. Doing this tends to cause more arguing between children and with you.
- Praise your children when they play well together. Children love to receive praise and this will encourage them to play well together. You might say, 'I like the way you are sharing your toys with each other.'
- Try to identify times of the day that seem to be worse for arguing. If bath time results in battles, maybe a period of separate bathing may be considered.
- Avoid spanking your children when they hit or fight. It confuses children to tell them they can't

hit when you correct them by hitting. Hitting children may teach them to hit others and might cause them to fight more.

- Try to spend time alone with each child. Sometimes sibling rivalry is a result of children trying to get your attention. Giving them positive attention may help solve this.
- Avoid comparing your children with each other. This can be hard if your second or third child is a challenge. Saying things like, 'Your sister always keeps her room clean, why can't you?' will only cause resentment between siblings. A child who is constantly being reminded of the good behavior of another child is certainly going to do their best to bring that child down a peg or two.

SIBLING RIVALRY – PARENT STORY

Jane and Mikel – four children aged six, four, two, and ten months

I am in the throes of grappling with this one with my second and third children, both boys. They were born on the same day two years apart. When the boys turned two and four things got a bit ugly. Mr four year old was very jealous of Mr two year old and wouldn't share, let him play, argued with everything he said, and was really mean to him. He generally has a lovely nature, and plays beautifully with his older sister and adores his baby brother.

All his anger was directed at the brother just beneath him. Well, I tried everything, modeling the appropriate behavior, songs, stories, ignoring, time out, separating them, placing them together, and nothing has worked.

Just the other day I said to my husband that we are going to be positive and tell our four year old that he is going to have a great day; that we know he will use kind words, share nicely, play happily, be caring, and loving to everyone. Every time he did something lovely, especially to his younger brother we would say, 'See, we knew you were going to have a wonderful day.' We would really play it up how happy we were and how proud we were of him.

So far we are up to five days of wonderfulness and tonight the four year old said, '(two year old) can come into my bed and listen to my bedtime story.' Will wonders never cease? We will continue with our wonderful daily praise.

Talking back

As a parent, it is frustrating to hear your own child answering back, name calling or using bad language. Luckily, with a little understanding and self-restraint, parents can put a lid on talking back. Firstly, try to find out *why* the child is behaving in this way. The child could be hungry, tired, frustrated, a victim of bullying, or copying older siblings. Keep in mind that when kids talk back, something else is going on underneath. The goal is to help them express it constructively. Below are some strategies that could help to clean up your child's act!

Avoid yelling, talking back or getting angry yourself

If you do this then you are reinforcing the behavior. Your child is angry, frustrated, or upset about something. Try to find out what is the root cause of the problem. Do not make it a bigger problem.

Communicate with your child

When your child backchats you, let him know that you care about his feelings, even if you do not approve of the way he is expressing them. Acknowledging your child's emotions can often diffuse the situation and stop it from becoming a big scene. If you can get past the attitude, you may be able to sort out what is going on and come up with some solutions.

Let your child know how it makes you feel

When your child has calmed down, let her know how her behavior makes you feel. For example, if your child shouts, 'I hate you,' you could explain that you love her very much and hearing those words hurt your feelings. You do not need to make a big deal out of it, but it is important to let children know their words and behavior can affect others.

Share the problem-solving process

Ensure your child understands that there are choices he can make about his behavior. If he is unable to listen because he is so angry or upset or defiant, then try talking about it later as a family. Role-play some scenarios. As a family, talk about what could happen next.

Children learn bad words before they learn the meaning of them

As hard as it is, try not to react to your young child swearing. Some children may delight in saying the word just to get a reaction out of an adult. Children may innocently repeat something they have heard or be unsure of its meaning. If it is a one-off incident, it is probably best to ignore it. Your child does not know what she is saying and chances are she will not repeat it again. If it becomes an ongoing problem, ask her what the word means then briefly explain why it is not acceptable.

Tell your child firmly that you do not accept bad language

Your child may begin using bad language consistently and in context. If used to express frustration, give him an alternative word. Have fun choosing descriptive words to use – for example, rats, jeepers, pumpkin, chocolate bananas ... Be careful not to use bad language yourself.

Apologize when you overreact

Model what your child can do when she overreacts or says things she does not mean. If you make a mistake, make it better by saying, 'I am sorry that I shouted and called you a bad girl. I was frustrated that you would not pick up the toys, but that is no excuse for calling you names.'

'No!' is a common backchat

If you are constantly hearing 'No!' then think about how you are phrasing the instruction. For example, 'Are you ready to go home now?' (when leaving a friend's house) is almost asking for a 'No!' Try instead, 'We are leaving in five minutes,' followed by 'We are leaving now.'

You simply cannot avoid disagreements with your children

However, you can have *rules* for disagreements:

- Don't attack.
- Don't belittle.
- Don't condemn.
- Define what the problem is.
- Define how to rectify it.
- Figure out what can be done to prevent it. in the future.
- Make up your own family rules.

Broken-record approach

Be consistent and fair with what you will and will not tolerate. Repeat why you find the behavior unacceptable. Try to remain calm and repeat it numerous times if necessary. Your child will get the message eventually.

Reward good behavior

Ensure your child is rewarded and congratulated when she is having a good day (or hour). Congratulate good behavior; let her know you are noticing when she chooses not to ask, 'Why?' or say, 'No!'

Be firm, consistent, calm, and loving in dealing with your child's misbehavior. Reassure her that it is the behavior that is unacceptable, not her. In the end, always give a hug and tell her how much you love her.

TALKING BACK – PARENT STORY

Nelly – two children aged four and three

Both my boys are very defiant and like to question *everything* I ask them to do. Star charts worked well. As a family, we try to focus on the positive behavior and not the negative. I attended an anger management course for parents recently and that helped a lot. It gave me a few strategies to deal with my emotions. My boys push me to my limits on a daily basis!

Temper tantrums

Tantrum behavior can start as young as around your child's first birthday. When tantrums first appear, many parents question what they have done wrong! In fact, temper tantrums are a good sign – they show your child is on target developmentally. Children this age need to be able to assert their independence. Sometimes this is expressed in temper tantrum behavior. Not only is this frightening and frustrating to you, but it is also a little scary for your child. Stay calm and offer him a hug when it is over.

What is a tantrum?

Many children show their frustrated feelings by screaming and kicking. Young children become frustrated because they lack the words to say what they are feeling, and therefore, they express their feelings in action – for example, temper tantrums. Tantrums often occur because a child is too tired, over-stimulated, or stressed. The result is an unplanned outburst of emotion.

What are tantrum triggers for your child?

If your child has a lot of tantrums, it is wise to record a 'tantrum diary'. Write down what may be triggering the behavioral outbursts as that way you can begin to come up with strategies for dealing with them appropriately. Note whether your child was:

- Tired.
- Hungry.
- Frustrated or unable to do something.
- Being refused something or feeling a sense of loss.
- Being rushed.
- Trying to be independent.
- Over-stimulated.
- Disappointed.
- Feeling misunderstood.
- Eating certain foods.
- Reacting to parent-stress.

Strategies to stop tantrums happening in the first place

Hopefully, you've worked out which triggers are causing the tantrums, and you and your partner have sat down and discussed some ways of doing things differently. Here are some tips to consider:

- Tired, hungry children are more likely to have behavior issues. Where possible, ensure your child is well fed (for this age group it is a good idea to take snacks and drinks with you when you go out), and well rested.
- Look for early warning signs, then distract or control the situation by offering choices.
- Set the stage for success by making activities simple and achievable.

- Know your child's limits. Challenge him, but try not to set him up for failure.
- Give him plenty of praise.
- Catch him being good.

If you consistently have behavior problems in supermarkets or other places, try to avoid going there with your child. Or, if you must, make the visits short. Make him a helper, or distract him with food, a toy, or a story while shopping.

Strategies for dealing with tantrums

If you've done your best, but the tantrum still occurs, try some of the following strategies:

- Stay calm (or pretend to).
- Ignore the behavior if you can. Sometimes tantrums stop if there is no audience.
- Set clear limits. Think about setting up routines and sticking to them. For example, if you want to buy your child a treat every time you go to the store, that's fine; however, if you don't, then it is probably best to never buy a treat. Children find it hard to understand that what is okay one week is not okay for the next.
- Whenever possible, help your child express her feelings in words: 'You really wanted mommy to buy that toy, didn't you?'

- Remove her immediately if she is hurting herself, others or property.
- Distract her. Children of this age can be easily distracted.
- Hold her close, and talk calmly and quietly in her ear. Calmly assure her: she is safe, you are in charge and you will not continue what you were doing unless the behavior stops. It may take time for your child to be consoled and back in control, so be patient but do *not* give in to the behavior.
- Tantrums in public can be embarrassing, but if you say 'No', then mean it. It is very important to be consistent with your approach. If a child learns that a certain behavior works then she is likely to try that strategy again.

Tantrums are common in one- to four-year-old children. They decline as children develop more effective ways of dealing with feelings and communicating their needs. Be consistent with your approach in dealing with temper tantrums, and try to have other family members adopt the same methods. We feel embarrassed when a child has a tantrum in public, and we are afraid of what people might think. It is important that we don't give in. If we do, then we teach a child that she can get away with things in front of other people. You can reduce tantrums and help your child (and you) to deal with stressful situations by using some simple strategies and sensible planning. Good luck!

TEMPER TANTRUMS – PARENT STORIES

Josie and Phillip – one child aged four

Our son usually saves his best dramatic performances for when we are shopping in public. We never take him out when he is tired or hungry, and we try to limit the outings to short visits. It helps if we calmly tell him what is happening before we go and what behavior we expect. Occasionally we offer a reward if it's a special event.

Petra and John – two children aged six and one

Our eldest child used to scream and kick when she had a temper tantrum. I would simply scoop her up in my arms, hold her close and leave the room or area. After she had calmed down, I would give her a hug even though I was usually seething with anger. I'd explain that I was unhappy with her behavior and that she needed to use her words if she was having unhappy or confusing feelings. Her tantrums were at their worst when she was three and by the time she started school, she was rarely having them.

> **Jane and Mikel – four children aged six, four, two, and ten months**
>
> To avoid tantrums I do try to always be consistent, set my rules as reasonable, and follow through with any consequences. If I ask children to stop an undesirable behavior – for example, 'Please keep your feet still or I will take you out of that cart,' and they do it again – I take them out. This usually produces a big reaction but they know that I will follow through with what I say and generally, they will listen. I never threaten what I can't follow through with – for example, 'If you do that again I'm canceling your birthday party.' Unrealistic and unfair!

Whining

Children do what works. If whining gets a reaction or attention from you then they'll continue with it. Eventually it becomes a habit and your child will find it hard to communicate any other way. To help teach whining children to talk in a normal voice try the following ideas:

- Every time your child whines ask him to use a 'normal voice'. He needs to know whining is not a normal way of talking. Model how you would like him to talk. For example, 'Mommy, could I have a drink please?' (instead of 'Mooommmmmyyyy, I'mmmmmmm thiiiiirsssty').

- Talk to your child about what whining sounds like. Give him an example – be humorous not mean about it. It may be he doesn't realize what he sounds like.
- Be consistent in your mission to stop whining. If whining works, your child will use it.
- Whining behavior may be reduced if you praise your child when he is behaving how you would like him to behave. For example, 'I really liked the way you used your normal voice to ask for a drink,' or even just, 'Great asking!'
- If all else fails, take a break with your child and do something fun like go for a walk in the park or read a book together.

WHINING – PARENT STORY

Jane and Mikel – four children aged six, four, two, and ten months

Well, this one drives me nutty! My daughter is the chief offender and she does it because I am sure she knows that it gives me high blood pressure. She has been doing it since about four, she is now nearing seven, and it is only just improving. We always try to ignore it or say

'Use a happy voice,' and often she goes and sits in her room until a lovely voice comes back to visit. If she is coming down with some illness, it can rear its ugly head. Daddy is very good at jollying her out of her whine session.

CHAPTER FIVE

Changes

Kim Masters, MD

Helping young children cope with changes, whether hopeful, such as moving to a new house, or a mixed blessing, such as the birth of a sibling, or sad, such as the death of a grandparent requires attention to the same four issues:

- Knowing the situation.
- Knowing the family.
- Knowing the child.
- Knowing what is known about the experience.

Knowing the situation

Ralph Waldo Emerson profoundly observed that no change is without its gains or its losses. This means that introducing a child to a new situation requires attention both to what is gained, and to what is lost. Unsuccessful changes result in anger and sadness rooted in what has been lost. Successful transitions, however, end with a sense of hopefulness about what is going to happen next.

Knowing the situation means understanding both verbally and visually, and if relevant in a tactile way – feeling and touching, what is going to happen. For example – if you are to explain a first time school bus ride, it would be important to know when the school bus is coming, the location of the stop, what the bus looks like both inside and out, where the child will sit, what to do during the ride, how to get off the bus, and what the destination (presumably school) will look like. Although young children learn in auditory, visual, and tactile modes, the latter are the most powerful in helping familiarity and comfort. Using the above example, learning about the situation could include visits to the home bus stop to observe a 'bus pick up', a view of the bus (both inside and out), a visit to the school to locate where the bus will arrive, and where the child will alight. Armed with this information, a parent can communicate the school bus ride experience, both by taking the child on a visit of all the above-mentioned sites and then having the child role-play the situation with a toy bus. Often a child will want to replay the bus trip until he feels comfortable with it. If this does not happen, then a parent can ask the child to show 'bus worries' to identify possible undetected fears. In general, repeated replaying of an event for a child is the same as an adult obsessing about a subject. In both cases, it indicates worry which needs to be discussed, or the underlying distress will not abate.

Some situations may not be possible for the child to visit, such as a move to a new house far away. In this case pictures of the house, with particular focus on the child's and parent's rooms are important. A 'play house' can then be used with the child to allow the child to experience the move, correct misconceptions that may be evident in the play, and answer unanticipated questions suggested by the play.

Some situations are difficult to describe, because they are at least partly unknown. For example, if a parent is taking a child to visit a sick relative, it may not be possible to know how the sick person will be dressed, what their house will look or smell like, what will happen during the visit. In these cases, it may help to talk to the child about several possible situations that could occur during the visit: for example, a brief visit to a bedside, a visit in the dining room which might include a snack, or a visit with a relative who is using a medical machine, like a portable oxygen tank. Using doll play, several options can be played out, while also showing the appropriate behavior desired from the child.

Knowing the family

The way children respond to a change is influenced *most* by the manner in which their parents respond, because they are 'in charge', and are responsible for modeling appropriate behavior and coping skills. If the parents are worried, their worry will be communicated to the child, even if nothing is said directly. If the parent is at peace about the change, the child will be also.

There is abundant literature on the destructiveness of intense 'expressed emotion' ('High EE') – that is, yelling, fighting, arguing, when trying to communicate. This means that trying to get a child to behave by yelling and arguing is not a useful strategy and in fact can destabilize interest in learning and promote fear instead. Arguing between parents in front of children also undermines the authority of the adults. Learning best takes place in a calm, safe-feeling environment. 'High EE' situations usually also reflect the stress of the parent and often occur as an act of desperation to 'make a child behave'. These situations should be anticipated and avoided. Failing that, removal of the child from the situation to a quiet and if possible, familiar setting, offers the best to bring about listening and behavioral acceptance of the parent's wishes. This result will be more likely if the child has discussed and played out the situation previously.

Not showing 'High EE', however, does not mean hiding feelings, because children will have a sense of unease, when assured that 'mommy or daddy is fine', when in fact they are stressed out, or sad. Emotional signals will come out despite one's best efforts. For example, if a mother is explaining that 'daddy is moving out' pending a divorce, this is best accomplished by playing out and discussing what is going to happen and admitting that 'this may make people feel sad or angry now, but in the future, we will make things calm down and the future will be safe'.

Through the use of dollhouses and puppets, the changes of a child and family during a divorce or other stress can be repeatedly played out.

Parents must also find visual and verbal ways to reassure fears that whatever happens between adults is not the fault of the child. This is a persistent issue which needs monitoring and often frequent discussion, because everyone, especially children who are involved, wants to be able to control outcomes.

Knowing the child

Different personality styles and experiences help shape our response to change. Children bring different traits to changes and transitions. A child who worries might have fears about his safety or that of his family when going away from home – for example, for a first day care experience. An impulsive child, on the other hand, may rush into the day care center and start acting 'wild' or oblivious of guidance.

Previous 'bad experience' also increases the expression of basic traits, because these coping styles are inborn approaches to situations. Suppose a child needs to get into a car and had previously been in a highway accident. However distress has been expressed in the past – refusal, clinging, agitation and so on – will present itself in amplified form in the car.

Anticipatory play games can help convert these distressing situations into hopeful experiences. An example is the 'New Baby' for playing out fears of a sibling's pending birth. In this game, a parent and the child sit next to each other with a blanket on their laps that can be raised over their heads like a tent. The parent makes the tent and tells the child that a new baby is coming. Then the child is encouraged to guess what the baby will look like. Peeking out from the blanket to try to visualize the new arrival often stimulates both curiosity and laughter. If the game is helpful, the child will want to repeat it as different ideas about sibling arrivals emerge.

Knowing what is known

Networking with family and friends about how to manage transitions can often be helpful, but if the suggestions differ, it can also be confusing. Fortunately, the internet is a great source for evidenced-based information. Using an internet search including the phrase 'evidenced based' can often provide novel information about any preschooler transition from first day at school, to moving house, to attending a wedding, or dealing with a crisis. You may also find useful information in discussion groups and forums.

Institutions that are routinely involved in transitions, such as schools, churches, moving companies, and state or federal courts, will often have suggestions about helping children.

A parting observation

Transitions promote both gain and loss, but it is their management with intrinsic hope and optimism that has always been the basis for triumph, resilience, and meaning in life. A young child's life should be the initiation into this process.

Kim J. Masters, MD

Kim has been a certified child and adolescent psychiatrist for over 25 years and during that time he has worked with families and children across the spectrum of psychiatric illness. He served for fifteen years as the Director of Youth Services for Appalachian Hall Hospital in Asheville, North Carolina. He was medical director of Focus by the Sea, a general psychiatric hospital in St Simons Island, Georgia. There, as Assistant Clinical Professor of Health and Behavior, Medical College of Georgia, he taught medical students psychiatry and treated both children and adults in an in-patient and out-patient setting.

Currently he is Medical Director of Three Rivers Midlands Campus Residential Treatment Center, where he teaches psychiatry to Physician Assistant Students and is Clinical Assistant Professor in the College of Health Professions, Medical University of South Carolina.

In 1992 he wrote a book, *Angry Child: Sleeping Giant or Paper Tiger.*

He represents the American Academy of Child and Adolescent Psychiatry to the Professional and Technical Committee of the Joint Commission.

Separation and divorce

When our lives take an unexpected turn and we find ourselves facing separation and divorce, one of our greatest concerns is our children. How will they cope, how do we organize parenting arrangements, how do we tell the children we are separating, and will I lose the children?

For many families, separation and divorce is an emotionally devastating time, where parents find themselves acting in ways that are not rational or cooperative. Children react more to the way their parents handle the separation (this includes parental behavior and emotional well-being), than the actual situation of a parent leaving. Like you, children need time to work through it.

Children love both parents equally and nothing will change that. Criticism of one parent in front of the children forces children to side with the criticized parent. This may not happen immediately, but it may as the children mature. The more the parents of children separating respect each other the easier it is for the child.

As caretakers of our children, a child's sense of self-esteem and self-love is supported when each parent is respected by the other. Children have attributes of both parents, so being respectful to the other parent results in your child feeling deeply respected and cared for. They can continue to take what they need emotionally and physically from both parents and thrive on knowing that both their parents acknowledge the love they had for each other (and therefore them). What is between the parents needs to remain between the parents.

In situations of separation when the parents take good care of themselves, their stress levels, their emotional well-being, their bodies (eating correctly), and maintaining respect for each other, then the children will easily find their way. They will continue to feel supported by both parents, and benefit from the wisdom of parents taking responsibility for their emotional responses.

Staying or going

Children cannot keep parents together. Often parents think that they stay for the children, but this is never really the case and other reasons are involved. Making children the reason parents stay together puts huge pressure on children, making them feel responsible for the parents staying together.

Although you are no longer partners, you will always be parents: you will always be the child's parent, despite remarriage, conflict, divorce, or criticism.

Children love both parents equally

Children are loyal to both parents and love them equally despite all that may have happened. Talk openly about what is happening but not the reasons why; wait until they are older for this. Tell them in ways that a child understands, with stories, drawings, and soft toys. As you are doing this, stop to check their understanding. Sometimes children misunderstand why or how this is happening. They may think it is only temporary, or that it is somehow their fault. Some activities could involve drawing a picture together – this may help them develop a new frame of reference that is positive and progressive for them and that includes both parents.

Recognize the signs of stress in a child

Children do not always communicate in words, but often express themselves through behavior. Recognizing signs of stress gives you an opportunity to help support your child through this transition and seek help if necessary.

Some signs of stress include:

- Afraid to leave either parent.
- Extra clingy.
- Frets for the other parent,
- Has no sense of time – hours seem like an eternity.
- Cranky and unsettled more often.
- Cries more often.
- Traumatized by long periods of separation from the principal parent.
- Developmental problems.
- Regresses to baby talk.

Ways to help your child cope

Children are becoming a little more independent of their parents, however separation can still be a major crisis for them. They may react with shock or depression demonstrated in behaviors such as change in sleeping habits, toilet habits, or deterioration of language and listening skills.

- Be patient and give them extra reassurance, give them only short breaks from the primary caregiver to begin with.
- Let them sleep with you when they are clingier.
- Take time to reconnect by reading stories and joining in with their play.

- Try to develop a routine. This helps children feel as though they have control over their environment.

Children in this age group still experience a short period of time as being a much longer time than it is for an adult. They are often confused by times and days. For example, an hour can seem like an eternity to a two year old.

- For older children, make a calendar together showing when they will be with either parent. Stick to these times where possible.
- Routines help so the child knows what is happening and when.
- Start with short breaks from each other – for example, ten minutes. Tell them when you will be back and be on time. Then extend the time over a period; this way children get to trust that you will return.

Children understand the world through different thought processes and make up stories or fantasize about things they do not understand.

- Provide reminders for the child of the other parent, using photos and toys given by that parent. (These special comfort toys can be taken with them when visiting.)

- Use healing stories to help create a healing picture within the child's soul to support their understanding. The 'Monkey Tree' or 'Mother Moon' in *Healing Stories for Challenging Behavior* by Susan Perrow deals with separation anxiety.

Children are very sensitive to ongoing conflict between parents. This is one of the critical factors affecting children's adjustment. Children become anxious, stressed, and depressed before staying with or visiting the other parent.

- Do not argue in front of the children.
- Children do not need to know the details in the early stages about why parents separated. They do need to know where they are going to live, who is going to look after them, and when they will see the other parent next.
- Providing a stable and safe environment will assist in easing anxiety.
- Share the better parts of your relationship with your former partner with your children.
- Get support to help you deal with any anxieties.

At times the child's behavior may be disproportionate to the situation. This is where feelings in relation to the family situation are perhaps being played out or displaced onto other situations. For example, prolonged crying over being refused one more cookie has little to do with the cookie and more to do with how the child is feeling about the whole situation.

- Take time – be empathic, creative and patient.
- Play, act, dance the feeling out, turn it into an animal, give the child permission, and oneself as a parent, to express the feelings in a safe and supportive environment.
- Ask the child to name an animal for how they feel and together dance it, exaggerating the feeling. For instance, dance the lion (the roar, the fierceness, and outrage), the little mouse (quiet, tender and vulnerable), the hippo (grumpy and big) and many more. Children know what they need to express.
- Children need time to adjust, so don't try to force a child to adjust to changes too quickly. Watch how they react to time with each other and adjust times through negotiation accordingly.

Pick-up and drop-off times

One of the most emotionally stressful times for a child is when a parent arrives to pick up or to drop off a child. Children are aware of the tension between the parents: they have experienced the shock and sadness too, and may feel insecure about further conflict and tension.

To help support children, you can give them advance notice of any changes, and show up on time and as planned. This gives children a sense of security – they can know and trust what will happen next. Keep to the arrangements as children can easily feel rejected and confused by unexplained failure to arrive or be dropped off at the expected time.

Visits

Visits are *not* times for parents to check up on each other or attempt to negotiate contentious issues. Children need to be able to go between both households without being questioned about what is happening in the other. Children will naturally want to talk about the other parent – but should not be 'pumped' for information. This distresses a child.

- Children need access to both parents, therefore helping contact visits remain positive and stress free assists in relieving further grief to the child.
- It is better not to move children between households too close to their bedtime. Nor is it beneficial to the child to start out on an activity or outing the minute they arrive or return. Allow the child to settle and adjust.
- Children may sometimes show distress in one form or other upon returning from seeing or staying with the other parent. The distress is usually real and a calm, empathic response will

help children work out their own way of coping with their parent's separation. Active listening allows the space for children to tell you in their own way what is going on, if they are aware of it, and then to begin to work through it themselves.

Different environments

Parents do not need to provide duplicate environments for their children concerning rules of behavior and so on. On the other hand, just as when both parents lived together, it is important to reach broad agreement on matters of child-rearing practices. It is not uncommon for there to be disagreements between parents about what is good or safe for children or other child-rearing issues. Effectively finding ways to support children through working together will benefit their adjustment. Give each other time to settle before trying to negotiate changes.

Things to avoid

Children are loyal and trusting of both parents. Therefore, as their parents, do not behave in ways that abuse their trust or take advantage of them:

- Using children as messengers between the two parents teaches children that adults cannot talk honestly or directly to each other.

- Anger between parents has a destructive effect on children – and often covers deep hurt and grief.
- Asking child to report on the other parent is destructive; it is using a child for your own ends.
- Do not use visits just to give the child a good time: outings and gifts do not take the place of normal parenting.
- Do not set up competing activities, as it spoils children's pleasure in being with either parent.

Children have a right to:

- Be loved by both parents.
- Be able to enjoy the love of both parents without excessive demands placed upon them.
- Feel proud of both parents and to be able to respect them.
- See their parents behave towards each other with at least minimal courtesy, consideration, and respect.
- Be listened to by both of their parents so that their needs are met.

As parents, if we can have respect and hold all the people in our life dearly, then we can intuitively guide our children into developing confidently and becoming able to meet many of life's challenges.

Judy – three children aged six, three, and two

Consistency in parenting styles proved to be problematic between my partner and myself in a shared custody arrangement. What was acceptable behavior in my partner's home was unacceptable in mine. Manners, dinnertime rules and general behavior slipped, and I found myself engaged in constant reminders.

To resolve the issue, my partner and I discussed the problem. We tried to come up with some rules that we both agree upon and would both apply when the children were in our care. We also spoke to the kids to explain that certain behaviors are acceptable and expected. When the children were doing as we asked, we used praise and encouragement to reinforce the desired behavior.

Did it work? Eventually – if we expect kids to be consistent in their behaviors, then we as parents need to be consistent with ours.

Moving

Moving to a new home, especially if it is any distance from the old one, is an upsetting experience for young children. They tend to like to do the same things in the same way day after day, and losing the old familiar surroundings is not a pleasant experience for them. They have difficulty remembering the old home in any but fragmentary ways – little bits and pieces – and this, too, can be frightening for them. The new home, even if nicer than the old, is not likely to look so to the young child at first. Here are some things parents can do to help reduce the upset and confusion.

Visit the new house

If possible, take the children to see the new place regularly before you move. This will help them get used to their new surroundings. Take a picnic and eat lunch there. One family even had their children take a few daytime naps in the new house before they moved in properly. Your child may be able to choose bedrooms and get to know the layout before you move. If you cannot physically go to the house, then see if you can view the house online – some real estates offer a 'virtual tour'. It is not the same as going there, but it is better than nothing.

Starting a new preschool or day care

Your move may allow your child to stay at the same preschool, but this is not always the case. If your child will be starting at a new preschool or day care, try to time the move for school holidays or, better yet, before the beginning of the school year. Leaving old friends and familiar teachers can be hard. If you are able, get the contact details of a few children at the new preschool or day care and arrange a play date – this way, your child may get to know at least one child before starting at a new place.

Involving the children

Let children help with the move. Let them pack some of their own things – or even better, carry their favorite things themselves from the old house to the new. This will help to make the transition smoother. They may also be able to take part in decisions about where to put the new furniture for their bedroom. When in the new house, have your child help you unpack their things, especially the things they use every day. This will help to avoid the inevitable, 'Mommy, where is my …?'

Getting help

Let them have some part, but try not to have them around throughout the whole process. Moving is an exhausting experience even for adults. It can also be dangerous for young children – large items of furniture being moved about and children don't mix. There is also the problem of items that are normally locked away becoming accessible. Have a neighbor, friend, or family member watch the children while you are doing the main part of the packing and moving.

Saying goodbye

Some people like to have a party or ceremony to say goodbye to the old house. This can be a way to help children work through their feelings about leaving. Remember to take plenty of photos of your children at the old house, as they will some day make wonderful memories.

Setting up in the new house

Try to make the child's new room as much like the old one as possible, even if it isn't the best arrangement for the new room. The child will be reassured by the familiar relationship among things, and once you have all settled down you can slowly rearrange them if it seems necessary.

Routines

Remember to use your established routines when you get to the new house. For example, even if the bedrooms are different, children will be comforted by knowing the going-to-bed routine is the same.

Staying safe

Remember that neither you nor your child knows where all the dangers are in the new house at first. So be extra careful and watchful for a while after you move.

The pressures around moving time may cause children to go back to behaviors they may have grown out of, such as bedwetting, thumb sucking and so on. This is normal and they will usually return to regular behaviour when they settle in.

MOVING – PARENT STORY

Jane and Mikel – four children aged six, four, two, and ten months

We have had to move house four times in the last three years, so I have had plenty of practice with this one.

- Children notice and will react to your stress levels. If you are stressed about the move then they will also be stressed.
- Be positive. Point out the good points of the new house and talk it up. For example, 'Aren't we lucky we are moving to a house with a big yard ... closer to grandma ... and so on.'
- If possible, take the children to visit the new house and look around.
- The last couple of times we have been lucky enough to have access to the new house before we have to leave the old house. This means the move can be spread out over a couple of weeks.
- Our moving essentials include kitchen basics (clearly labeled), enough clothes for a week packed in

suitcases, toiletries, and the children's toys and 'blankies', and these are the first things to be unpacked.

- When I am packing, I try not to do too much in the day – with four young children this can be anything from impossible to dangerous. I also don't want them to become too unsettled by changing their routines. I do most of my packing when they are asleep.
- To make things easier during and after the move I try to make extra meals (about two weeks' worth) ahead of time and freeze them.
- When we are in the new house, we make a point to explore the house, yard, and neighborhood as a family. This allows us to check out what is safe and to establish new rules if need be.
- As a family, we stick to the same well-established routines we have always had. I feel this helps the children to settle in and feel safe and secure in their new environment.
- I think the best way to go about moving would be to have the professional movers come in and pack up your whole house, then unpack it at the other end. This way you can take the kids to the beach or the park and life would be easy. I'm working on that for our final move!

Preparing your child for a new baby

Here are a few hints to help you prepare your other children for a baby brother or sister:

- Talk to your child about the birth of the baby. Tell him what the baby will look like, where the baby will sleep, and how babies act. Some young children have unrealistic expectations of what a newborn baby can do. I know one little fellow who was ready to play football with his new brother on the day he arrived home.
- Avoid asking your child if he wants a brother or sister because he may wrongly think that he can choose, and he may say, 'No thank you'!
- Answer any questions your child may have about you and your changing body or about the baby. There are some great picture books available for children that can help you discuss this.
- Let your child help you get ready for the baby by shopping with you for baby supplies or by helping you fix up the baby's sleeping place.
- If you are planning to move your child to a new room or into a bed, make sure you do it well ahead of the baby's birth.
- If your child does not have a baby doll get one before the baby is born – you can role-play how

to hold and act around a newborn baby. I know some dads are quite uncomfortable about their sons having dolls, but explain it will help the child to adjust to the new baby and it also helps young boys to role-play at being like dad!

- If you can, have your child spend some time around babies. Ask a friend or relative with an infant to visit.
- If you have baby pictures of your older child, look at them with your child and talk about what he was like as a baby. Read books about new babies with your child.

Helping your child once the baby has arrived

Children younger than four or five years are often jealous of their newborn brother or sister. Children react differently, and negative behavior is a sign that the big brother or sister is having trouble getting used to the new baby. This is very normal.

- When older children lose some of their parents' attention they will try to get it back any way they can. They may imitate the baby and start crawling or drinking from a bottle or wetting their pants again, all of which is very common.
- From birth on, talk about your new baby as a person. For example, 'Emily is crying. Do you

think she is hungry?' Researchers have found that when parents talk about the baby this way the older child can adjust to the new baby's needs.

- Let your older child help care for her new brother or sister. Siblings are more likely to help each other when this is expected of them. Ask them if they would like to help change or feed the baby.
- Spend some time alone with each child. There should be times when the child doesn't have to share you. This will help your child know that she is still loved.
- Give your older child her own 'baby doll' so she can imitate you taking care of the baby. Younger children really enjoy doing this. You may say to your child, 'I'll help you take care of your baby and you can help me take care of your little sister.'

NEW BABY – PARENT STORY

Antonija – five children aged seven, five, three, two, and six weeks

Whenever I am expecting a new baby, I let the kids be as involved as much as they would like to be and as much as is developmentally appropriate. If they feel comfortable doing so, I let them be the first to tell their friends, teachers, and relatives. My girls love to come shopping with me to choose a special outfit or toy for the baby. When they would come to visit after the baby was born, they would be surprised with a gift from the baby. (My son aged three, asked how did all of the presents fit in my tummy with the baby!)

I let my children show the baby as 'news' at preschool or kindergarten. At home, I encourage the kids to talk, play, and hold (in my presence) the baby. My two year old loves to give our six week old his pacifier and holds his hand. I put wipes and diapers in an accessible place and play racing games to see who can get them first when it is time for a change. I let the children help wash the baby and rub oil on his feet (I massage the rest).

I found that the most important thing was to let the other children know that they were still loved and appreciated. I made sure they understood the baby was not 'off-limits' – I feel this helps to avoid resentment.

Starting day care or preschool

Starting day care or preschool is a big step in a child's life, and for many children this will be the first time they have been apart from you. Children will react to this new experience in different ways, but almost all children will need some kind of support to help them adjust to the new situation. The following are suggestions for making this transition a successful one:

- Visit the center or preschool with your child to familiarize her with the environment. Show her around the room – point out where her lunch will go, where her bag is kept, and where the toilets are. Introduce her to the caregivers. Get down on the floor with her and let her play with the toys and the other children. Try to join in with the routine (story time or snack time). Some children may jump right in and others may hang back or cling to your leg. This is normal behavior. The idea is to build up trust and make her feel safe.

- Talk to the staff about your child – for example, what she likes to do, successful ways of settling her to sleep, foods she likes and dislikes. Explain any fears or special needs (out of earshot of the little one would be best).
- At home, read your child books about starting childcare. Role-play by pretending to be mommy, daddy, child, and caregiver; practice saying 'Goodbye' and coming back. Talk about the caregivers and the children at the center as well as some of the fun things you did when you visited. Talk about or draw pictures about what your child might do when she visits next time.
- If you will be working while your child attends day care or preschool then take your child to your workplace and show her where you will be while she is away from you.

- Try to keep the first couple of days shorter – for example, until lunchtime. This will give her a chance to bond with the caregivers, get to know some other children, become confident with the routine, and settle in.
- It may help to let her take along her favorite blanket or cuddly toy.
- Create a leaving routine. For example, give your child a cuddle then guide her to a staff member, or sit down with her for a short playtime or book reading together. When you are ready to go, tell her that you are leaving and that you will be back to pick her up at the end of the day. Give her a kiss and a hug and say goodbye – then leave. *Never* sneak away from your child. Learning how to separate from a parent is an important skill. Your honesty will build your child's trust in you.
- Some children settle in quickly and others take a little longer. A preschool teacher for sixteen years states, 'Some children will always have trouble separating, but are fine for the rest of the day. They just need support during the "goodbye" phase.'
- When you pick her up, she will most likely be quite emotional. This is understandable – she has been away from you all day and now she is letting it all out with the person with whom she feels the safest.

- Acknowledge your child's feeling about being away from you. These feelings are real. It is okay to say, 'It's hard to be away from mommy. You miss me. I miss you too.' Take time to examine your own feelings – if you feel comfortable with the center, your child will be too.
- Last of all, when you get home take the time to learn about her day (if she is willing to share) or just play with her. This will make the day care/ home transition a smoother one.

STARTING DAY CARE – PARENT STORY

Marika – one child aged two

We placed our son in day care when he turned one but he was always very clingy so I made the decision not to go back to work and just stay home. If I had to go to a meeting with my husband, I would leave him with my mother and he would become so upset that I had to stay home. When he was two, I decided to go back to work but I wanted the move to day care to be smooth for him and not traumatizing. At two he would cry if he couldn't see me.

I spoke to the director of the center and we organized visits for the days he was enrolled, one month prior to him actually starting. Mondays and Fridays I took him in the morning, would stay for about half an hour, and gradually lengthened this out to about three hours.

> I would gradually leave the room, so that by the third week I would sit outside reading a magazine.
>
> This worked well. He became familiar with the surroundings and his teachers, but also that when I dropped him off, I was going to come back. When he actually started day care, it was very smooth and not at all traumatizing for him. He jumped out of my arms and happily played. It couldn't have gone better.

Talking to your children about economic changes

Children are exposed to world events, including the downturn in the economy, through TV, radio, newspapers, magazines, and adult conversations that they overhear. The information can be scary and they often need help coping with what they've seen or heard. When you start talking with your children, you help them recognize their feelings and understand the situation.

More than anything, children need to be assured that they will be cared for. They will seek comfort in knowing that their parents are there to help them understand what is happening. Children are very sensitive about what is going on around them. They may be aware that things have changed, but are not sure why. They can develop all kinds of misconceptions when they have not been informed about what is happening around them. They may think they are being punished if new family budgets affect meals, outings, and treats. They may even be worried about quite serious things such as losing the house or having to change schools.

How do you reassure your children, help them to build resilience and to feel triumphant in these difficult times? Here are some ideas on how to help your children cope.

Talk about the events

Young children find it very difficult to understand the concept of money – to them you seem to have an infinite source. Explain to your children in the simplest terms why your family has less money to spend at the moment. How much detail you go into will depend on the age of the children. Discuss with your children what you as a family are doing to save money. Ask children how they feel about what is happening, and what their concerns are. Encourage them to say what is on their mind. Answer their questions and help them understand what's going on.

Brainstorm

Include your children in brainstorming sessions about how to save money. Some ideas may include always taking snacks and drinks when you go out to avoid buying them, joining the library to access books and games, and making homemade gifts. You may be surprised at what your children will come up with if they are given the opportunity. Including children in this process will help them to gain a sense of power and control over the situation.

It is a good idea to brainstorm a list of all the great things you have in your family's lives, both material and non-material. This will draw your children's attention to what they can be grateful for and not on what they are missing.

Monitor the media

Try to reduce your children's access to news programs. Although at times young children do not know what is being said, they do understand that something is wrong.

TALKING TO YOUR CHILDREN ABOUT THE ECONOMIC DOWNTURN – PARENT STORY

Misha and John – two children aged four and nine

It has been a tradition in our family to visit my folks in California each July. (We live in North Carolina.) We have done this every year since our first child was born. My husband and I are both teachers and this is something our family looks forward to months in advance. This year we have had to cancel the trip. My job has been cut back to two days a week and one of our cars will need replacing soon, so we just can't justify the cost. We knew the girls would take it hard, and they did.

We had a family meeting and explained in the simplest terms why we couldn't go to visit their grandparents this year. It was hard for our four year old to understand and she kept offering her pocket money to help out. We acknowledged the children's sadness and let them know it was okay to feel this way. A few days later we had another meeting to talk about what we could afford to do during the holidays. We decided to holiday at home and choose one day of the week when we would do something special as a family – we took turns to choose the weekly activity. My husband and I were surprised at their choices – we thought they would choose movies, the zoo and so on. Instead, they wanted to do things at home like build a birdhouse, bake, and look for tadpoles in the creek.

It has been a lesson for all of us, knowing we can make do with less and, in a way, I feel this experience has brought us closer together as a family.

Talking to your children about death

Just as birth and new beginnings are a part of life, so too is death and the loss associated with it. Talking honestly and openly to young children about death can go a long way in helping them to understand it and to develop positive coping strategies. Following is a list of ideas on how to approach this delicate subject:

- Death is a hard concept for young children to understand. It needs to be explained in a very simple concrete way. For example, when someone dies you can tell your child that the person is no longer breathing and their heart is no longer working. Let your child know that the person can no longer walk, talk, eat, or sleep. Children experience life in the here and now, therefore by explaining that the person's body is no longer alive and can't do the things such as walk, talk, and eat makes it a little easier to grasp.
- Often children will ask for this information repeatedly, particularly if it was someone close to them. Young children struggle with the idea that death is permanent and not reversible. Children have very vivid imaginations so if they imagine the person is still alive then they begin to question the permanency of death. Always answer questions calmly and simply.
- If a family pet dies (which is always so sad), this can also be a time of learning. Allow your child to calmly observe the stillness of the pet's body. Point out that there is no longer any movement or breathing. Explain to your child that the pet's body is no longer alive. Include your child in any rituals or belief systems you may have about death. This can provide a framework for

understanding what death is and how to cope with it.

- Talk to your child about your belief systems (if you have any) surrounding death and remember to keep your explanations simple. Answer any questions your child may have or ask your child if he has any questions.
- After explaining about death to your child, you should ask him to explain it back to you. It is remarkable what can be uncovered when you do this! He may come out with something completely different from what you have just said. Often these differences are made up of misconceptions that your child has about what death is. Therefore, it is necessary to gently correct any misconceptions. You may have to go through this explaining and repeating it back process several times. Not all at once – this may occur over several days or even weeks. Just have patience and gently go over the same explanation each time and try not to alter your explanation as this can cause further confusion.
- Find some children's books that explain the concept of death, read them together and answer any questions that your child may ask.
- If it was someone close to your child who died, it can be helpful to put together a special book

about this person. Use photographs and encourage your child to draw some pictures or tell you what to write about them. You could ask your child what were his loved one's favorite things to do and include these in the book.
- Encourage your child to express any feelings that he may have and let him know it's okay to feel sad or angry etc.

Some common misconceptions young children can have about death

- Death is not permanent.
- Death is reversible.
- Magical thinking (imagination) – for example, 'I was angry with Auntie Dot and wished that she would go away and that's why she died.'

Basic concepts that help children understand death

- Universality – the concept that all living things eventually die.
- Irreversibility – children struggle with the idea that once the physical body of a living thing is dead, it can never be alive again.
- Causality – young children are challenged with understanding what it is that really does or can bring about the death of a living thing. This is

where young children's vivid imaginations come into play.

- Non-functionality – this refers to the end of all bodily functions such as breathing, eating, walking, and playing.

TALKING ABOUT DEATH – PARENT STORY

Amanda – two children aged four and three

Earlier this year our family experienced the death of a great aunt. The children asked lots of 'why' questions about her illness. Aunty was sick with a brain tumor and we always tried to be honest with them about what was happening, without going into too much detail. We would simply describe what was happening to her and when it was clear she was dying, we let them know. We didn't want to hide it from them as I could tell they knew something was going on. After she died, we answered any questions they asked. My youngest had trouble understanding that her death was permanent, so we read him a book called *Lifetimes* and that seemed to help him understand.

CHAPTER SIX

Fears and Anxieties

Dr Ross Campbell

Most adults find it difficult to comprehend just how powerful and real the fears of small children are. If only our long-ago memories were a little fresher, if only we could feel again just how it was to be in a large, unfamiliar world with so little information to help the moment make sense.

We grown-ups cope with our own fears and anxieties, of course, but we are armed with greater resources for managing them. In particular, we have advanced reasoning facilities and considerable experience with the world. However, your two- , three- or four-year-old child is not so well equipped. That's why we parents need to anticipate the sources of those difficult emotions.

What does a preschool-age child fear? The list could be nearly endless, but we can round up a few of the 'usual suspects':

- *Darkness* – fear of the dark is amongst the most ancient and common of all fears; something of an iconic childhood event. Slightly open closets and oddly shaped lamps can seem menacing to a little one.
- *Separation* – around the age of two, a great many children become very anxious about any type of separation from the parent – typically from mommy. Try dropping off a child of this age at Sunday school, or at the childcare center, and the usual tantrum may brew.
- *Strangers* and general unfamiliarity – small children, normally active and talkative, will grow shy around unfamiliar people. It's common to see them hiding behind the parent's legs or a chair. We expect the mall Santa Claus to offer a delightful encounter, but it may be a fearsome one.
- *Imaginary threats* – everyone knows how vivid and expressive the imagination of a child can be. Without an adult's ability to reason and understand, the child's line between the rational and the imaginary can be a very fine one.
- *Loud noises* or commotion – unexpected clamor or confusion will prove unsettling for a two- , three- or four-year-old child. That's why we try to keep our children in quiet, safe environments as frequently as we can.

- *Animals* – you and I recognize that the romping beagle is simply being playful, but things look different from a height of 35 inches.
- *Parental fears* and anxieties – children are highly sensitive and emotionally acute. When adults become anxious or fearful, children immediately take on those same feelings. The adult is the source of safety and meaning; if they become uncertain, then the child's world has suddenly been robbed of its foundation.
- *Objects under the bed* – many children imagine frightening objects under the bed during the night. Simple ways to help your child with this problem are to look under the bed and assure the child; have the child look under the bed himself, or simply assure the child that all is well.

We observe a category of children in this age group who are particularly shy and dependent upon the parent. Mom and dad naturally worry about the child's reticence; they wonder if this is a case of special needs. It may be, but it's also true that many children – like many adults – simply need a bit more time to become acclimatised to anything or anyone new. Shyness isn't necessarily the same as fear. More often than not, parents will find that patient love will help the child learn to venture cautiously out from the 'safest adult' to the next safest, until separation anxiety is no longer an issue.

Anxiety is a bit like fear, but a special category thereof. Anxiety is fear without a face, the uncomfortable semi-awareness that life lacks equilibrium for whatever reason. Fear of darkness or the babysitter is specific and can be handled accordingly, but a child's anxiety may come from a source more difficult to determine, or indeed from several sources. The child may become silent, temperamental, particularly needy of affection, or the child may manifest some other behavior. The watchful parent will note the change in behavior and avoid the trap of also becoming anxious. That response, of course, will only lead to more anxiety for the child. A cycle of anxiety can escalate.

As we'll see in the next section, the best response is to offer unconditional love and enhance the child's feeling of safety and security.

Responding to the child's fear and anxiety

The primary need of any child is to feel unconditionally loved and accepted. So many of the child's fears – separation, unfamiliar circumstances, and the parent's fears, for example – can ultimately be seen as threats to the child's basic, foundational sense of having a home and being loved there. Some children say they're afraid of the dark, for instance, when the real issue is aloneness. At bedtime, the child is asked to go away from mommy and daddy and actually fall asleep that way.

This is why it's not enough simply to love our children. We must be certain that we affirm that love in every way we can, as often as we can. When children are afraid of the dark or fearful of bedtime, we affirm that we're right nearby, perhaps on the other side of a wall or door. We're slightly apart, but our love is intact. We also spend special time with them before bed, reading a story, embracing warmly, and 'loading up' that special affection between parent and child.

It's important to speak patiently and compassionately with our children when they express a fear. 'A monster? That's silly!' is a distancing statement rather than a reassuring one. Sometimes all the child needs is for the adult to listen, and for the opportunity to verbalize the fear. That in itself might cast out the fear.

We also need to be very conscious of what children see and hear, and how they perceive that information. Mommy and daddy may speak in terms only half-serious about 'being poor' or unable to pay the bills; nevertheless, the child hears this as a true threat. Where will he sleep? Will the toys be taken away? Some dads joke, 'We'll just throw you away!' or 'We're going to give you to another family,' with that traditionally masculine, aggressive jocularity. The child may not detect the nuances of grown-up humor. Parents can never forget that little ears perceive and hear a different world.

Above all, the issue of security is central in helping the child grow beyond normal fear. At all times, we want our preschool children to know they have a permanent home and loving parent(s). Darkness will only last a few hours, until the morning; the babysitter is only here a few hours, and mommy or daddy will return. The parents must establish themselves as strong, affectionate, and available to help with whatever seems threatening or uncertain at the moment. The Bible tells us that perfect love casts out fear, and that statement is never truer than in the case of parent and child.

Dr Ross Campbell

Dr Ross Campbell discovered his life's calling more than 30 years ago. He found himself fascinated by the inner dynamics of child development, and particularly by the crucial relationship between parent and child. He compiled a simple manual that identified, in plain language, the basics of good parenting. Ultimately, this effective manual found its way into the hands of publishers. The result was *How to Really Love Your Child,* a book that experienced phenomenal sales numbered in the millions across the world.

In subsequent years, he has added books on parenting in special areas such as teenagers. His book,

How to Really Love Your Teenager, won the Gold Medallion Award. Other books included *Helping Your Twenty-Something Get a Life and Get it Now.* He even wrote a volume for grandparents. Dr Campbell has also written extensively on dealing with anger in children; a subject he believes to be crucial. In collaboration with Dr Gary Chapman, he has authored the bestselling *Five Love Languages of Children.*

Dr Campbell is a former Associate Clinical Professor of Pediatrics and Psychiatry at the University of Tennessee College of Medicine. He has counseled thousands of parents over three decades of practice. Now retired from active counseling, he focuses today on writing and lecturing on parenting topics for an ever-changing cultural world with its challenges for the modern family.

Dr Campbell and his wife, Ann, live in Signal Mountain, Tennessee. Between them, they have seven adult children and fifteen grandchildren.

Fears

Young children can be fearful of all kinds of things. Common fears are storms, dogs, loud noises (vacuum cleaners, water going down the plug), strangers, and insects. Here are some tips to help you and your child through this stage:

- Stay calm when your child is afraid. Your child will look to you for your reaction. Staying calm will reassure her and make her feel safe.
- Let your child know that it is okay to feel scared. Try saying, 'You don't like the thunder,' or 'That loud noise scared you, didn't it?'
- Try not to go over the top with the attention you give to your child when she is scared. If you pay too much attention, she may think there really is a reason to be afraid. Tell her about something you were afraid of when you were little and how you grew out of it.
- Although it is hard, try not to pass your own fears on to your child.
- Talk to your child about her fears. She may have a misconception that can be cleared up. Tony explains, 'When our little girl was two years old she was afraid of the noise the water made going out of the bath. She told us she thought a monster lived under the bath and was going to get her. We were able to discuss it with her, and even looked down the drain with a flashlight to establish there was nothing there.'
- Try distracting your child with a toy or book. There are some excellent picture books that address common fears that you can read to your child.

- Play it out. Some children benefit from playing out the fear again and again. This lets her deal with her feelings in a safe way. If the fear is dogs, you and your child can take turns at being the dog and the child.
- If your child is particularly scared of something or someone, give her some time to adapt before going ahead. Start small – if your child is afraid of the vacuum cleaner let her touch it when it is off, she may even feel safe enough to 'play' at vacuuming. Move on to doing the vacuuming when she is playing outside with another adult and then maybe watching through the window.
- If you stay in sight, you can help prevent fears. If your child can see you, she will feel safer.
- Never make fun of your child's fear or get angry if her fear seems silly.
- Remember, childhood fears are a normal part of growing up.

FEARS – PARENT STORY

Misha and John – two children aged four and nine

When my younger daughter was two, she was very frightened of loud noises. Things like the vacuum cleaner, blender, or the lawn mower would upset her – she didn't even want to go near them when they were off. It was becoming quite a problem. We would try to use these things when she was not around, but it was not always possible. My husband saved the day! He found some industrial ear protectors he had lying around in the garage. She wore them when we used the 'noisy fings'. It worked! She thought they were great, they seemed to desensitize her to the noise. After a while she didn't need them anymore. Every now and again, she still asks for her 'quiet ears'.

Nightmares

A nightmare is a distressing dream that causes at least partial waking. Children may wake scared, anxious, and upset. Nightmares may start at age two and peak between ages four to six. Common themes are being chased by frightening persons (bad guys, witches, monsters), or animals (lions, tigers, bears). Nightmares seem to be a part of normal development and do not usually signify serious problems. They usually occur during the early hours of the morning, but each child is different.

Nightmares may be caused by:

- The ordinary stresses of childhood – at this age children are learning to deal with a variety of strong emotions, and the nightmares may act as a release of pressure for these stresses.
- Watching scary TV shows or reading scary books. Even the news, heard or watched, can depict frightening themes to children. Remember, what is scary to one child may not be scary to another.

- A traumatic event such as surgery or an accident.
- A vivid imagination.
- Fever.

What can you do if your child has a nightmare?

- Go to your child and comfort him by giving him a hug. Use a calm and gentle voice.
- Take his fears seriously. You and I know there is not a monster under the bed, but to a child recently woken with a nightmare it seems very real. You may like to check under the bed, but let him know it is for his benefit, not because you feel there is any danger.
- It may help your child to talk to you about his nightmare. Together you could think of a different and 'happier' ending for the dream. Putting the nightmare into words can make it seem less powerful; changing the ending can help your child to master his fears.
- Stay with your child until he feels calmer. If he is particularly upset, try quietly reading a favorite book or singing a song.
- The next day you could draw or role-play the nightmare with the new 'happier' ending. Allowing your child to play out his fears is a powerful tool.

Help prevent nightmares

Stick to an established bedtime routine. This is a great start to helping a child feel safe. I know one father who, as part of his children's bedtime routine, recites a little poem designed to keep away nightmares. It goes like this:

> 'Thank you for the day,
> And for the beautiful night,
> May I have good dreams,
> And sleep through the night,
> Thank you for the day.'

- Monitor your children's television and books. As adults, we tend to forget that most movies depict at least one baddie. What is scary to one child may not be scary to another.
- There are plenty of books you can read to your child that address the issues of nightmares and night fears. These types of books will help your child to explore and master her feelings and fears.
- Having a night light, keeping the door open, or sharing a room with a sibling may also help a child feel safe. If the nightmares are becoming more frequent or you feel something is not right, then seek help from your health professional.

Jane and Mikel – four children aged six, four, two, and ten months

Avoid watching television and be choosy about the books that you read to your children. Think about the images you place before them. My children have never had bad dreams or nightmares.

Jennifer and John – three children aged fifteen, eleven, and nine

When he was younger, our son came into our bed every night because of nightmares. To deal with this problem we stripped his bedroom completely (with his help). Cleaned every nook and cranny. Put only the essentials back into the room (with his help). That way he knew exactly what was in his room and he couldn't wonder what a spooky shape was in the middle of the night. We removed the large dinosaur mobile from his room. We went to the fairy shop and purchased some smooth 'sleeping' rocks for under his pillow and a beautiful dream catcher for above the head of his bed.

He still came in to my bed sometimes but not because of nightmares. He has never had serious nightmares since! We wished we had tried it sooner but I think the fact he was old enough to physically help me with the process was meaningful.

Monique and Chris – two children aged six and three

My daughter would wake up crying at night, but she couldn't remember what woke her up. I realized she was having nightmares and started to monitor how and why this was happening. I became conscious that my behavior was affecting her – if I was stressed or always rushing to get things done, there was a pattern of her having nightmares on those nights. On the nights when she would wake up crying, I would place one hand on her back and use the other to gently stroke her face. I would reassure her, then she would eventually go back to sleep. Life still gets busy, but when I notice myself rushing her, I try to slow down.

Shyness

There are many reasons why children are shy. Look carefully at the situations where this behavior is occurring. If play dates and parties are a problem area, then do some work at home to set your child up with some coping strategies.

- Teach your child how to enter and exit groups and how to read other people's body language. Role-play some scenarios at home; have older siblings or your partner assist to show different ways of interacting with people in a variety of situations.

- Help your child understand what it takes to make friends. There is a range of good storybooks available on the topic. Try reading these stories and comment on character's interactions in movies or on the TV show they are watching.
- Ensure you are role-modeling good social skills. Think about how you welcome people into your home. Focus on how you introduce people and make them feel welcome.
- Make a game of practicing social skills outside your home. Give family members points for saying 'Hello' and smiling at shop assistants, shaking hands or giving hi-fives when they meet people, and saying 'Thank you' when they receive something. Make a list of the types of behaviors you want to practice before you leave home.
- Arrange play dates for your child regularly. Try to make it the same day each week to give her a sense of routine. Start slowly with having one friend over for a play date. Suggest the child comes to your house first, so your child will feel more confident. Build up to more children once your child feels comfortable.
- Examine your expectations of your child when you go on a play date. Do you expect her to entertain herself immediately and leave you to talk with adults? Is this expectation fair and

realistic? Do you need to invest time settling your child in?

- Don't expect children to go off and play together straight away. You may need to sit down with your child and start her off with a toy or game until she feels comfortable. Praise any efforts she makes at playing near or interacting with other children.
- Seek out safe places for your child to interact with others (friends, relatives, playgroups, playgrounds, and libraries).
- Don't make a big deal of it if your child does not want to join in. Praise her efforts when she does communicate with others, but let her move at her own pace.

Some other points for you to consider

- Take things slowly. When in social situations, let her watch for a bit until she feels comfortable.
- Help your child identify interests and hobbies that make her feel special and use these to encourage play with other children. Help your child learn to manage her emotions. Talk about how she feels in these situations. She may let you know she feels overwhelmed. You can teach her to manage this by taking five slow breaths – practice this at home.

- Encourage gradual change and praise successes.
- Labeling your child as 'shy' can have negative consequences, so it is best to avoid using this label in front of your child. Saying things like, 'Oh, don't worry, she's just shy,' will send the message to your child that she is shy.

SHYNESS – PARENT STORIES

Linda – two children aged five and four

My daughter is very shy outside of the home. When we go out, I let her sit on my knee and then wrap my arms around her. I don't talk directly to her. I talk freely with adults and children around me. She knows that she can move away when she is ready, but she cannot monopolize my attention. She watches and observes from the safety of my arms. I don't tell her to go and play; I don't push her off my knee and place expectations on her, and she goes and returns as she wants. It works well with my daughter. Without exception she leaves me to explore or interact; sometimes it takes a while. I would only get tears and frustration if I forced her to interact.

Melissa – three children aged seven, four, and one

My son always takes a long time to 'warm-up' in social settings. He is often rude and aggressive, and this is because he is feeling self-conscious and shy. Unfortunately, his negative behavior usually ensures he gets more attention! I ask people not to focus too much attention on him until he is feeling safe and secure. This usually takes about ten minutes. Close friends and family know to 'ignore' him until he's ready to join in. I'm confident that he will outgrow it; as his older brother did once he started school. We do talk about when he does well, and I give him lots of praise whenever possible.

CHAPTER SEVEN

Media

Susan Mims, MD, MPH

Our world today is inundated with media. It is difficult to escape it, or protect our children from it (and should we?). There are many types of media, and within any type there is the good, the bad, and the ugly. What we really want to do as parents is offer the good to our children, while keeping out the bad and ugly. As they grow, we must teach our children to do this for themselves.

We know that reading to young children has many positive benefits. Children who are read aloud to show better language skills and school readiness than children who are not.[1] As long as the material is appropriate for the age of the child, reading is a good medium for children. Many parents sing their kids to sleep because it helps calm them down, or play child-friendly songs for them to dance to for exercise. Some music can agitate children, however, and music listened to through earphones has the potential to damage a child's hearing for life. Just like books, music can be beneficial or harmful.

Books and music are not the most common forms of media that come to mind when we think of children's exposure to media these days, though. Probably the first thing that pops into your mind is that good old TV that sits in the center of almost all households. Television permeates our lives. Ninety-nine percent of homes in the US have a TV, 66 percent have three or more TVs, and the average American watches four hours of television per day.[2] In a typical day, 75 percent of children under six watch TV and one in five children under two have a television in their bedroom.[3] In addition, children may be exposed to background media, such as the TV left on in the house all day.

Now we add computers into the mix; video games, internet, instant messaging, hand-held gadgets that can go anywhere. A 2006 Kaiser Family Foundation study of children younger than six years old found that 83 percent of these children use screen media daily and a 2005 Kaiser study of eight- to eighteen-year-old children revealed that kids spend nearly six and a half hours a day using media.[4] This means that most kids spend more time using media each day than they spend in all other activities except sleeping. In addition, just like adults, many children spend media time multi-tasking, using more than one form of media at the same time. This actually increases the total exposure during the same timeframe. Even our youngest children are the focus of media advertising and sales with TV shows, DVDs, and computer games marketed specifically for infants.

What is all of this exposure to media doing for our kids? The answer is still being researched, but it seems to come down to content and duration. Numerous studies document the harmful effects of exposure to television violence and violent video games on children. Children, especially the very young, show signs of fear and anxiety after watching violent or scary shows. Seeing violence acted out on screen can desensitize children to real-life violence and can even cause some children to become aggressive. So, the answer is simple, right? Just do not let your children watch shows with violence. Well, that may not be as simple as you thought. The National Television Violence Study conducted between 1994 and 1997, found that two out of three TV programs contained violence and these shows averaged six violent acts per hour.[5]

So, we know that violence in the media has been lurking anywhere for quite some time now. What else is out there to disturb our children? Another content area not appropriate for children is the sexuality displayed on TV and the internet. A study conducted in 1996 found 8.5 sexual interactions per hour during the first hour of prime time; the so-called 'family hour'.[6] Even more striking is that this figure more than doubled since 1986, and this trend has the potential to increase, affecting our children even more so today. Anyone who has searched for something on the internet knows that sexually explicit sites can pop up in the least expected places. In addition to exposure to sexual content, media can expose children to tobacco, alcohol, and illicit drug use and unhealthy body images.

The inappropriate content in media is not the only bad thing that should concern us. Advertising exposure often promotes unhealthy behaviors. Children are exposed to more than 40,000 ads each year just on television.[7] From one-quarter to one-third of television programming consists of paid advertisements and this seems to be increasing.[8] The Kaiser Family Foundation reports that nearly half of all TV ads are for food and the vast majority of food advertising consists of ads for candy and snacks, sugared cereals, fast food, and soft drinks. Children learn to recognize brand logos as young as age two or three, and advertisers target them to develop brand loyalty from an early age. All of this junk food advertising is likely contributing to the increasing obesity epidemic among our children. Not only does this advertising promote unhealthy eating habits but it also results in children wanting food at times when they are not hungry thus causing them to eat more. In addition to increased caloric intake, television watching often replaces time spent in more invigorating activities resulting in fewer calories expended.

While companies spend less on internet and video game advertising than on TV, these ads appear to be ever increasing in prevalence and taking a more interactive approach. 'Advergaming' is a new term to describe the myriad free video games targeted to children on the internet. The cost to companies is far less than television spots and the children have repeated exposure, reinforcing the message, while playing the game over and over. These websites are usually kid-friendly and therefore may not be blocked by parental internet filters.

Given all of these concerns about media, why would a parent want to expose a child to it? Some studies demonstrate beneficial effects of watching television. Children can learn basic language skills while watching educational shows or videos. Video games targeted to specific age groups can teach math or reading. The internet offers a wealth of information at your fingertips. Children can answer any question they have, learn about cultures around the world, and learn new skills from the internet. In addition, media can be great entertainment.

So, how can you protect your children from the bad, yet offer them the experience of the good in media? The American Academy of Pediatrics recommends that all parents become media-literate and teach media literacy to their children.[9] Media literacy involves analyzing the messages and images in media. Labeling the purpose of an advertisement or identifying product placement in movies or on the internet helps empower the media user to objectively consider what they are viewing. Parents who are media literate can make better media choices for their children. However, since media is such an integral part of our lives from a very young age, media literacy should be incorporated into everyday life, as part of a child's other education.

The child who is well media-educated will be able to limit media use, make positive media choices, choose healthy and creative alternatives to media use, develop critical thinking and viewing skills, and understand the implications of media on social, emotional, political, and economic behaviors.[10] Many studies are now demonstrating that media education can reduce the harmful effects of media for children.

Because children under two years old need human interactions to develop their social, emotional, and cognitive skills, the American Academy of Pediatrics discourages all television use in this age group. For children older than two, parents should do their homework before exposing their children to media. Carefully select programs and watch with your child. Look for opportunities to teach media literacy as you watch. As children are growing up, watching television as a family can open opportunities to discuss what you see. It may just promote good family communication, but it may also present opportunities to talk about educational topics. Remember to turn off the television during meal time. This will also promote family communication.

Choose carefully what you and your child watch. Remember you are your child's role model. The TV ratings published by the TV Parental Guidelines Monitoring Board can be helpful. When you research a show ahead of time, you can check its rating in your guide. The rating can also be used with a V-chip, a standard component of televisions since 2000 (although you might not know it); to restrict what type of shows can be viewed from the set. You will likely find this function labeled 'parental controls'. Even after you enable the parental control on your television, you still must be alert to content. Some researchers have expressed concern that these ratings are becoming more lenient over time, potentially exposing younger children to content not appropriate for them. Movie ratings are also helpful but with the same cautions.

Monitor your child's internet use. Put the family computer in a central location where you can view the screen as you move about. Set time limits on media use and stick to them. Offer alternative activities that involve imaginative play and physical activity. These are critical to healthy child development. The American Academy of Pediatrics recommends no more than two hours of non-educational screen time per day. This allows time for other activities. Make your child's bedroom an 'electronic media-free' environment. Read to your child as often as you can. You will both enjoy it.

Susan Mims, MD, MPH

Dr Mims is the Medical Director of Mission Children's Hospital in Asheville, North Carolina. She leads Mission Children's Hospital as it grows to meet the healthcare needs of children in western NC and to promote children's health throughout the region. Prior to joining Mission in 2006, Dr Mims worked for six years with Buncombe County's public health department and the largest provider of indigent care in the county. She served as the county Medical Director, leading disease outbreak investigations as well as overseeing the clinical work of the department. Prior to coming to Asheville, Dr Mims practiced primary care medicine in Durham, NC.

She received her medical degree as well as her Masters in Public Health in Epidemiology from UNC Chapel Hill. Dr Mims continued at UNC Hospitals for a combined residency in Internal Medicine and Pediatrics. She also completed a Preventive Medicine Residency at UNC. Dr Mims is board certified in all three specialties. While working and living in Asheville, she is very active in many national, state, and community health organizations and spends time advocating for children's health issues. Dr Mims enjoys living in Asheville with her husband and two sons, aged ten and eight.

Media literacy

What can you do to help your child become more media literate?

Young children have difficulty distinguishing between programs and commercials. To help them to learn the difference you can play the 'What are they trying to sell?' game. If you allow your children to watch commercials have them try to guess what the commercial is trying to sell. This game can help to teach your child that selling is the only purpose of a commercial.

Another way for children to develop media literacy is to get them talking about what they are watching. During television programming or movies, ask children, 'Who is telling this story?'

- A four year old may identify the main character.
- A five year old may realize there is a narrator.
- A six year old may be able to understand that the narrator is a story-teller.
- An older child will eventually grasp the concept of writers making up stories for TV.

Ask your child to re-tell a story that she learned from media. This is not to check for accuracy but rather to encourage your child to think and discuss what she sees and hears in media.

Ask your child to name some things in the background. This can help build the concept of a constructed set.

Ask your child to describe how music makes her feel. This can help introduce the concept of media producers using sounds to influence how people react to their media.

MEDIA LITERACY – PARENT STORY

> **Nicola and Rob – two children aged six and three**
>
> I try to make a habit of watching TV with my children occasionally. It is amazing how many questions they ask when I sit with them! Many of the questions seem to be about whether things are real or not. I try to explain in simple terms what is happening – for example, that the person is dressing up as a witch and is not a real witch. We have even dressed up and made our own 'TV show', which has really helped our six year old begin to understand what happens in the movies or on TV.

Choosing appropriate electronic media

As parents, we need to protect our children by monitoring what they watch, as well as educating them to become media literate.

Movie ratings

Pay attention to ratings and use them as a guide, but be sure you are aware of what is depicted in a show or movie before allowing your children to watch. Even movies that are rated G contain images and themes that are frightening to young children. Remember that you are the best judge about what is or is not appropriate for your child. Think twice about asking friends and relatives about the appropriateness of movies or TV shows unless you know you have similar views – what they think is appropriate and what you think is appropriate may be two completely different things. If in doubt, watch it yourself before you decide if it is appropriate for your child.

What movie ratings mean

- **G rating – General Audiences. All Ages Admitted.**
  This signifies that the film rated contains nothing most parents will consider offensive for even their youngest children to see or hear. Nudity, sex scenes, and scenes of drug use are absent, violence is minimal; snippets of dialogue may go beyond polite conversation but do not go beyond common everyday expressions.
- **PG rating – Parental Guidance Suggested. Some Material May Not Be Suitable For Children.**
  This signifies that the film rated may contain some material parents might not like to expose to their young children – material that will clearly need to be examined or inquired about before

children are allowed to attend the film. Explicit sex scenes and scenes of drug use are absent, nudity, if present, is seen only briefly, horror and violence do not exceed moderate levels.

- **PG-13 rating – Parents Strongly Cautioned. Some Material May Be Inappropriate For Children Under 13.**
  This signifies that the film rated may be inappropriate for pre-teens. Parents should be especially careful about letting their younger children attend. Rough or persistent violence is absent; sexually oriented nudity is generally absent, some scenes of drug use may be seen; one use of the harsher sexually derived words may be heard.
- **R rating – Restricted. Children Under 17 Require Accompanying Parent or Adult Guardian.**
  This rating requires accompanying parent or adult guardian (the age varies in some locations). This signifies that the rating board has concluded that the film rated contains some adult material. Parents are urged to learn more about the film before taking their children to see it. An R may be assigned due to, among other things, a film's use of language, theme, violence, sex, or its portrayal of drug use.

- **NC-17 rating – No One 17 and Under Admitted.**
  This signifies that the rating board believes that most American parents would feel that the film is patently adult and that children aged seventeen and under should not be admitted to it. The film may contain explicit sex scenes, an accumulation of sexually oriented language, or scenes of excessive violence. The NC-17 designation does not, however, signify that the rated film is obscene or pornographic.

Review websites

There are some great websites that will review and break down what is in movies for young children so you can decide for yourself if it is okay. (See 'Resources' at the end of the book.) Have a good look around these sites and check out movie reviews of movies you already know. This way you will know which site best suits your idea of appropriate viewing.

TV ratings – V-chip for television

The Federal Communications Commission requires that all televisions made after 1999 that are larger than 13 inches include a V-chip. The FCC explains that the V-chip allows parents to block television programming that they don't want their children to watch. Most television programs are now assigned a rating according to a system established by the broadcasting industry. The rating is encoded with the program so that, using the remote control, parents can program the V-chip to block from viewing shows with certain ratings. If you lose your remote or need help programming the V-chip, contact the manufacturer of your television for a replacement remote or for instructions on how to operate the V-chip.

Ratings appear in the corner of your television screen during the first fifteen seconds of each program. The ratings are also included in many magazines and newspapers that provide TV listings. Ratings are given to all television programming except news, sports and unedited movies on premium cable channels. There are six possible ratings:

- **TV-Y** (All Children) found only in children's shows, means that the show is appropriate for all children.
- **TV-7** (Directed to Older Children) found only in children's shows, means that the show is most appropriate for children age seven and up.
- **TV-G** (General Audience) means that the show is suitable for all ages but is not necessarily a children's show.
- **TV-PG** (Parental Guidance Suggested) means that parental guidance is suggested and that the

show may be unsuitable for younger children. This rating may also include a V for violence, S for sexual situations, L for language, or D for suggestive dialogue.

- **TV-14** (Parents Strongly Cautioned) means that the show may be unsuitable for children under fourteen. V, S, L, or D may accompany a rating of TV-14.
- **TV-MA** (Mature Audience Only) means that the show is for mature audiences only and may be unsuitable for children under seventeen. V, S, L, or D may accompany a rating of TV-MA.

The best way to check if something is appropriate is to watch with them

If your child is watching something for the first time, watch with them. You can then monitor what your child is seeing. Some children will alert their parents if they are scared of something they see, others just internalize their feelings.

Don't be afraid to turn the TV off or walk out of the movies. If you or your child feels uncomfortable then don't watch. Listen to your instincts – children may tell you they are not scared, but if you feel what they are watching is not appropriate then act on those feelings.

Nicola and Rob – two children aged six and three

I must admit I get a bit frustrated with movie rating and movie makers in general. Most of the content in G-rated movies seems fine, but why do so many of them seem to include a scary 'baddie'. I also dislike the way many characters put each other down. Many G-rated movies contain the word 'stupid' – I don't want my daughters to hear, or learn to say this word.

Setting limits with screen time

There has been a lot of discussion about the diet and exercise habits of American kids. Most families are now seriously looking at how much 'screen time' their children are getting on a daily basis.

During the summer holidays, after school, and on weekends, television and computer entertainment can be a great way to give kids 'downtime'. It's often easier for you; they're quiet and entertained and you're able to get chores done. Use these tips to help limit the amount of time your family spends in front of a screen:

- Set a time limit for each child in your family. Try using a simple chart to track screen time. Each day give children their allocation of screen time. With young children you may wish to draw (or print off and cut out) a TV program icon, such as *Blue's Clues* and *Dora the Explorer*. Do the same with video games and computer use.

- Some young children find the transition from watching television or playing video games to a different activity difficult. This is especially true for video games where there is not necessarily an 'end' to the game. The child wants to keep playing to better his score. They can become angry and frustrated and it is tempting to let them go a little longer. Have an activity ready for after they have finished – read a book to them or go for a bike ride together. Be consistent – if they know you are serious about time limits they will be more likely to accept your boundaries.
- Keep the television off when you have finished watching. This seems like common sense, but many parents of young children have the TV going constantly in the background.
- Limit your own screen time. Set a good example. Try recording your own favorite shows to watch after your kids go to bed and try to avoid spending extended periods on the internet or playing video games.
- If you have older children in the house, make sure they know the rules. Talk about what programs and games their younger siblings are allowed to watch

or play with, and for how long. Sometimes young children can sneak into an older sibling's room and become involved with inappropriate activities or discussions, or slip in extra viewing time.

- Control the number of screens you have in the house. The fewer screens, the easier it is to monitor.

Hey, even Bill Gates sets screen-time limits for his three children! Bill and his wife Melinda have limited their seven-year-old and ten-year-old children to a total of 45 minutes a day of total screen time and an hour a day on the weekends. This is in addition to what their oldest child needs to do on the computer for their schoolwork.

Have a family meeting and discuss *why* you are setting screen limits. As a family, decide what is fair and make a list of all the other activities your children can do once they have used up their precious screen time!

SCREEN TIME – PARENT STORY

Ingrid and Brad – two children aged seven and two

The amount of time our younger daughter watches TV varies from day to day. The days we are at home together, she may watch two to three 20-minute DVDs. The three days she is in day care she may watch one 20-minute DVD when we get home. My husband and I have the same views on television viewing. We don't like her to watch too much, although we have never had to enforce limited time as after about 20 minutes she will head off to do something else. We are always aware of what she is viewing as we make sure we are in the same room.

Computer use

In this section, we will look specifically at the issue of the computer and your child.

When looking at the development of young children we know that they need to interact with people, they need to handle objects in their physical environment and they need to solve open-ended problems. In a nutshell, computer time cannot solely enable your child to achieve these developmental goals. However, like other toys and tools within your child's reach, the computer is likely to work well when it extends natural play. Most parents are unsure if computer use is necessary for preschoolers.

There has always been controversy regarding whether computers are appropriate for young children. Interestingly enough, research has shown that computers are being used in the majority of day care centers. Although some authorities in the field of early childhood education believe that computer use interferes with development, many day care directors disagree. If you decide you want your children to have limited use, then make it part of their play. They need many opportunities to make decisions, to take turns, and to gain mastery over an activity. Although you don't want your children staring at the computer for hours on end, you do want them to make the most of their time there.

Recommendations about computer use with young children clearly state that they should be monitored while they are on the computer. At home, ensure the computer is in a family space and not in an office or bedroom. Adults in the home need to visually monitor computers being used. Preview all games and programs your child is going to view. Use one of the many family filters or parental controls available to help keep out nasty content – but remember these are not foolproof. If the internet is being used, we recommend you sit beside your child and supervise fully.

Make sure you ask lots of question as your child is using the computer. Although it is tempting to walk away if she is happily amused, try to sit down and ask your child about the games and activities she is doing. Ask questions about how to play the game, who the characters are, what is happening, and what happens at the end.

Try introducing your child to websites and programs she will find interesting and which will inspire her with creativity. There are multitudes of programs out there. Let them scrapbook photos, write their name and simple words, send emails to family and friends, check out TV characters' websites, and Google a question.

If your child is attending a day care center or being cared for in another home, find out how the computer is utilized. Often day care facilities are taking a leadership role in enabling children to access technology that otherwise might not be available in the home.

- Ensure your child is supervised adequately and preview all material used (use media ratings as a guide).
- Promote exploration and play and the basic computer skills needed, such as using a mouse.
- Don't let computer time substitute for physical activity.
- Be careful about using computer time as a reward for good behavior or using the computer in free time (as an electronic babysitter).
- Establish time limits and be consistent.
- Teach media literacy.
- Provide lots of non-media activities for your child.
- Be a positive media role model yourself.

COMPUTER USE – PARENT STORY

Monique and Chris – two children aged six and three

Our older child has access to a computer and she started using a computer at the age of three and a half. She indicated an interest in using the computer when she would see me typing letters or sending emails. She would ask if she could send an email too. I only allow her to use educational programs on the computer and limit her time to no more than an hour. I believe that using the computer is a positive thing, as it is going to be something she will use often in the future. Children need to learn about technology. Putting a limit on her time has worked – once her time is up we move on to doing an activity outdoors or read books.

I believe that if I didn't set time limits, along with carefully monitoring what programs she uses, then the computer could have a negative effect on her. As she gets older, I will allow her more time on the computer, but will always monitor what she is doing.

Video-game use

Does your child have access to video games?

If you decide to let your child play with computer or video games, ensure you take the time to preview what he is doing. Is the game appropriate? Is there a media rating?

When your child is using the game, resist the temptation to sneak away, leaving him with his electronic babysitter. Ask your child lots of questions about the game. Your questions will get your child thinking more.

Instead of buying a low-priced game, try to think about your child's interests and buy a game that complements his interest. Play it yourself first. Are there varying levels of difficulty? Is it challenging? What is the plot?

Look for games and activities that give your child opportunities to express his preferences and interests, rather than having everything preset by the software. The freedom to select a color or a character at the beginning of the game, as well as the chance to make other choices throughout the play, will develop your child's independence and sense of control.

Being able to set the skill level allows your child to begin in an open-ended 'explore' mode. As he masters the program, he can then move on to more challenging levels at his own pace.

Try to choose games that allow multiple players. Playing a computer game or program with another child or perhaps yourself will give your child a chance to talk about what he is learning and discovering. You'll find out what he is thinking.

Avoid games that promote stereotyping. Subtle gender and cultural bias may be engrained in some activities. A character's voice, for example, may connect a certain accent to a negative behavior.

Other tips:

- Limit how much time your child plays electronic games.
- Try not to use them as an electronic babysitter.
- Don't use them as a reward or free time activity.
- Encourage physical and social play activities.

- Avoid games whose characters use violence to resolve conflict.
- If possible, borrow or rent a game prior to buying it. You can then check it out carefully to see if it is appropriate for your child.
- There are many independent reviews available (many online) on games, so do some research.
- Some games can be 'addictive' to children. Monitor usage, be proactive and stop or restrict usage if necessary.
- Ensure older siblings know what the rules are regarding their games and younger siblings.

Electronic Game Ratings

- **Early Childhood** – titles rated **EC (Early Childhood)** have content that may be suitable for ages three and older. Contains no material that parents would find inappropriate.
- **Everyone** – titles rated **E (Everyone)** have content that may be suitable for ages six and older. Titles in this category may contain minimal cartoon, fantasy or mild violence and/or infrequent use of mild language.
- **Everyone (Ten years +)** – titles rated **E10+ (Everyone 10 and older)** have content that may be suitable for ages ten and older. Titles in this category may contain more cartoon, fantasy or

mild violence, mild language and/or minimal suggestive themes.

- **Teen** – titles rated **T (Teen)** have content that may be suitable for ages thirteen and older. Titles in this category may contain violence, suggestive themes, crude humor, minimal blood, simulated gambling, and/or infrequent use of strong language.
- **Mature** – titles rated **M (Mature)** have content that may be suitable for ages seventeen and older. Titles in this category may contain intense violence, blood and gore, sexual content, and/or strong language.
- **Adults Only** – titles rated **AO (Adults Only)** have content that should only be played by persons eighteen years and older. Titles in this category may include prolonged scenes of intense violence and/or graphic sexual content and nudity.
- **Rating Pending** – titles listed as **RP (Rating Pending)** have been submitted to the Electronic Software Rating Board and are awaiting final rating. (This symbol appears only in advertising prior to a game's release.)

Endnotes

1 US Department of Education, NCES (2006), The Condition of Education 2006.

2 www.csun.edu/science/health/docs/tv&health.html. Accessed 10/26/2008.

3 Kaiser Family Foundation, *The Media Family: Electronic Media in the Lives of Infants, Toddlers, and preschoolers, and Their Parents*, May, 2006.

4 Kaiser Family Foundation, *Generation M: Media in the Lives of 8-18 Year-olds*, May 2005.

5 Center for Communication and Social Policy, University of California, Santa Barbara, National Television Violence Study, Volume 3, 1998.

6 Kunkel D, Cope KM, and Colvin C for Children Now and the Kaiser Family Foundation, *Sexual Messages on Family Hour Television: Content and Context*, 1996.

7 American Academy of Pediatrics Policy Statement on Children, Adolescents, and Advertising. PEDIATRICS Vol. 118 No. 6 December 2006, pp. 2563-2569 (doi:10.1542/peds.2006-2698)

8 Kaiser Family Foundation. *Shouting to be Heard: Public Service Advertising in a Changing Television World*. January 2008.

9 American Academy of Pediatrics Policy Statement on Media Education. PEDIATRICS Vol. 104 No. 2 August 1999, pp. 341-343

10 American Academy of Pediatrics Policy Statement on Media Education. PEDIATRICS Vol. 104 No. 2 August 1999, pp. 341-343

Conclusion

By combining the generations of knowledge and experience on offer from the child development and child health expert co-authors and myself, I am delighted at what we are able to offer in *The Triumphant Child – A Practical Guide to Raising Two, Three and Four Year Olds*. As parents, we have a responsibility to ourselves, to our children, and to our society that we evolve with each generation to become better parents, availing ourselves to improved and more reliable resources. I would like to extend heart-felt congratulations to you for using the magnificent resources that *The Triumphant Child* is offering you. You have made the choice to become a proactive parent, allowing your natural inherent parenting skills based on love, nurture, and gut feelings, to be supported with traditional tried-and-tested techniques and fresh, new approaches that work!

About Sixty Second Parent

Sixty Second Parent is a platform that connects parents with knowledgable experts in the fields of Child Health, Child Development, and Practical Parenting. The www.SixtySecondParent.com website was launched by Dr Olson Huff MD, a nationally acclaimed pediatrician, after he recognized a need for a clear and easy way for parents to access easy-to-understand professional parenting advice that can be trusted. We acknowledge there is really no such thing as a 'Sixty Second Parent', that caring for children is a full-time job. However, by visiting the website, parents will be able to learn new tips and strategies to support their parenting.

Olson Huff believes that providing parents with practical, relevant, and timely information is more important than ever in today's society.

Along with practical parenting tips and information, site visitors have access to reviewed products in the online store, they can ask questions of an online panel of early childhood specialists, and participate in online parenting forums. In addition to the support offered by the site, parents can receive a copy of the newsletter packed with practical parenting information from leading experts in the areas of parenting, baby, toddler, child health, and development.

Resources

Sixty Second Parent • **www.sixtysecondparent.com**

US Department of Education • **www.ed.gov**

The American Academy of Pediatrics • **www.aap.org**

Safety Net • **www.safetynet.aap.org**

Center on Media and Child Health • **www.cmch.tv**

Kaiser Family Foundation • **www.kff.org**

Substance Abuse and Mental Health services • **www.samhsa.gov**

The Center for Disease Control • **www.cdc.gov**

National Institute of mental health • **www.nimh.nih.gov**

Food Pyramid • **www.mypyramid.gov/kids**

National Network for child care • **www.nncc.org**

MOVIE REVIEW SITES

www.parentpreviews.com/index.php

www.dove.org/default.asp

www.commonsensemedia.org/

www.kidsfirst.org/

Acknowledgments

We express sincere gratitude to the following content contributors who have graciously shared their knowledge and experience to add significant value to this book:

Chapter Authors

Anne Oxenreider

Margaret Taylor

Nicole Rawson-Huff

Dr Olson Huff

Dr Kim Masters

Dr Ross Campbell

Dr Susan Mims

Content Contributors

Tracey Richardson

Michelle Hutchison

Brenda Sutherland

US Department of Education

Parent Stories

Jane and Mikel
Antonija
Ingrid and Brad
Monique and Chris
Helena and Joe
Jen and Rich
Nadia
Ted and Michelle
Bess
Lily
Chantelle and Taj
Catherine
Crystal
Marnie
Melissa and Ben
Judy
Matthew
Melissa and Dave
Nelly
Josie and Phillip
Petra and John
Marika
Amanda
Misha and John
Jennifer and John
Linda
Melissa
Nicola and Rob

Copyright Acknowledgements